In the
BLINK
of an
Eye

FORGIVENESS
in Black and White

In the BLINK of an Eye

FORGIVENESS
in Black and White

JT CLARK
AND
TERRI LEE CLARK

Trilogy Christian Publishing

Trilogy Christian Publishers

A Wholly Owned Subsidary of Trinity Broadcasting Network

2442 Michelle Drive
Tustin, CA 92780

For information, address Trilogy Christian Publishing

Rights Department, 2442 Michelle Drive, Tustin, CA 92780.

Trilogy Christian Publishing/ TBN and colophon are trademarks of Trinity Broadcasting Network.

For information about special discounts for bulk purchases, please contact Trilogy Christian Publishing.

Manufactured in the United States of America

10 9 8 7 6 5 4 3 2 1

Library of Congress Cataloging-in-Publication Data is available.

ISBN#: 978-1-64088-145-7

ISBN#: 978-1-64088-146-4 (E-book)

Dedication

This book is dedicated to the memory and legacy of my brother and his wife, Bobby and Pam Clark. May our Father in heaven be glorified by the telling of this story. May it have an eternal impact on the many people who read it.

grow through, what you go through

Original artwork by: Jordan Nallen

Foreword

Forgiveness is at the heart of the Father. When I look at the life and story of J.T. Clark, I see the love of the Father. Being a pastor for over 20 years has given me the opportunity to listen to many testimonies of how people came to faith in the Lord Jesus Christ. Several years ago, I was asked to speak at a police conference in Virginia. It was then that I met J.T. for the first time. When I heard his testimony during this conference, it truly resonated with me as a story that was genuine and authentic! I could tell he was not a seasoned minister. As he shared his story, what I heard was life-changing!

Walking through hardships and difficulties in life could either ruin a person or bring them to a place of healing and wholeness. I believe in every person's life there is a time when they are confronted with the reality of God. How they choose to respond is up to them.

I know what you are about to read in this book has the power to change and heal the hearts of those who read it. J.T. and Terri Lee Clark are genuine and authentic followers of Jesus Christ. The story has so much strength and resolve in it. Walking in obedience is always a choice. The Bible teaches us that the steps of the righteous are ordered of the Lord. This means being in right standing with God. This comes when we surrender our lives to His Son, Jesus Christ. My prayer for all who hear the story of J.T. Clark's road of forgiveness is that it will play a huge part in leading people towards the Savior, Jesus Christ.

It is a privilege and honor to be able to prepare you for what you are about to encounter in the calling and path that God has placed on J.T. Clark. May the Lord richly bless you and strengthen you, as you embrace this story of love, forgiveness, reconciliation, and healing.

Andrew Columbia
Pastor, Chaplain, Author, and Trainer

Preface

I don't believe in coincidences. I never really did. Truthfully, I just never considered them much. Beginning in August 2015, a series of events would unfold that put things in a much different perspective for me. The confluence of circumstances in my life that would come together on the night of August 21, 2015, and then continue to unfold in the years ahead, could not be explained in the natural realm, especially if there is no such thing as coincidence.

The story that you are about to read is almost too much to be believed, especially if you don't believe in God. On the surface, one might think the details are just too incredible and could only be made up by a Hollywood screenwriter. But these things did happen and continue to happen.

I encourage you to read the pages ahead and open your spirit up to a world of possibilities. Where people of different races, backgrounds, and interests unite around a tragic accident. Where the key ingredient ends up being love. Hearts and minds are transformed through an outpouring of grace and mercy. The lives of the people taken from this earth continue to impact those who had been touched by their spirits while they walked amongst us.

See how God used a most horrific, tragic accident to move within churches, families — an entire community — to lift spirits and transform lives. Witness how He moved specifically in my life, telling me on October 7th, 2017, "Don't you understand? You are now experiencing testimonies of your testimony." Essentially, He was saying the entirety of this situation would become bigger than anything I could fathom.

It is hoped that through the pages ahead you will be touched and inspired to pursue life from an "in the world" perspective versus an "of the world" perspective. That you will seek to understand all that God intends for each person who desires a relationship. And, as appropriate, individuals will pursue changes that have eternal implications.

Acknowledgements

There are so many people to thank and acknowledge in the writing of this book. Certainly, love and appreciation go to my wife and three daughters. Terri Lee, Jordan, Caitlin, and Whitney spoke words of life and love to me throughout. On October 23, 2016, as Terri Lee and I were driving north on I-95 just south of Jacksonville, Florida, I looked at her and said, "If God has to send one more person to tell me to write a book, I don't know what I will do."

I also need to thank my family. My mom, Nancy Clark, my brothers, Norman and Sam Clark, my sister Susan Brown, my brother's children, Robin Quesinberry and Torrey Clark. Each of these people offered their support and encouragement as this process was completed.

To my House of Purpose (H.O.P.) family, you just don't know the impact you have had on my life. You live the expression of "Love God…Love People!" You have taught it to me. To my pastor, C.J. Martin and first lady, Fernanda Martin, to the elders and deacons, to the praise and worship team, to each person that calls H.O.P. home, thank you. Terri Lee and I love you.

To my brothers and sisters of T.R.A.S.H. Ministry, what can I say? I love each of you. You interceded on behalf of our family even before we knew there had been an accident. To my pastor, Mike Price, and first lady, Stephanie Reynolds-Price, thank you for your love, guidance and friendship. Mike, when I told you that I was not an author, you said, "I know of a few others who weren't authors either: Matthew, Mark, Luke, John, Paul. You get the point?"

To Dan and Sabrina Whitlock, thank you for continuing a friendship that began through Bobby and Pam. You were with them at the end of their race on this earth. I cannot imagine how painful and beautiful that must have been. You have opened your church to Terri Lee and me. You have encouraged us throughout this journey into ministry. Terri Lee and I love you both, dearly.

And to Andrew and Angela Columbia, who would have known that a last-minute, God-encounter would have led to an ongoing relationship of ministry, growth, development, and friendship? Terri Lee and I are grateful for the encouragement we have received.

Lastly, we would like to acknowledge Dave and Karren Schuller, Andrew Bandy, Neal Turner, Bob Suddarth, Joel and Terri Stuart, Mike Pruitt, Andy

Seastrom, and Lee and Dee Stiltner. Each of you have prayed for, critiqued, counseled, and encouraged us in one way or another. We thank you and we love each of you.

Table of Contents

CHAPTER 1

A JOURNEY BEGINS

JOHN 14:12 (KJV)

"Verily, verily, I say unto you, He that believeth on me, the works that I do shall he do also; and greater works than these shall he do; because I go unto my Father."

Plato, the ancient Greek philosopher, is credited with saying, "Necessity is the mother of invention." I believe that our advocacy is directly related to our experiences. Until you have been impacted by juvenile diabetes, or cancer, or heart disease, or know someone who has, most don't get too involved in such causes. If you don't have a passion for animals, stories about overcrowded shelters may not compel you to action. So it was with me.

Due to a myriad of situations, experiences, and circumstances, I had reached a plane of existence in my life where I pretty much wanted to be left alone. I loved my wife and children. I enjoyed the occasional interaction with a group of people. But if all I did was go to work and return home, that was enough for me. I struggled with relationships outside of those with my wife and children. I just wanted to be left alone. I did enjoy my work, especially now that I was involved in emergency management. I believed that I had something to offer in this new and growing field. This was particularly so in bridging the distance between local emergency management at the jurisdictional level and that of healthcare emergency management. Yes, between my current employment situation and the love of my family, I was feeling pretty good about things.

At the time this story takes place, my wife, Terri Lee, and I were preparing to celebrate our 28th wedding anniversary. We had raised three daughters, Jordan, Caitlin, and Whitney who were then 22, 21, and 20 years old respectively. All were students at different colleges across Virginia. They were my life.

I suppose this was the proverbial calm before the storm.

In the summer of 2015, I was ready to serve my ninth season as a member of the chain crew for the Franklin County High School football team in Rocky Mount, Virginia. For those who do not know, the chain crew is an extension of the game's officiating team. The chain crew is responsible for marking and tracking possession and downs on the field by using a set of chains attached to down markers on the sideline. That was generally my assignment. It was an opportunity that first began when we moved to this community from South Florida. Our daughters were entering the 7th, 8th, and 9th grades. I reasoned that they would want to go to the high school football games on Friday night, so I might as well find a way to get involved.

In 2014, a friend, Keith Scott, who is the director of facilities management for the school system in the county directly to our south, Henry County, Virginia, had children enrolled at Bassett High School. He learned that the chain crew for their football team was not returning for the 2014 season. He reached out to me to see if I could assist. I also volunteered as a member of the chain crew here in 2014 through 2016.

On Friday, August 21, 2015, the temperature was warm, and the weather was fair. The day was unremarkable by all accounts. Just a run of the mill summer evening.

Late in the afternoon, I met a colleague, Billy Ferguson, in Rocky Mount. We were carpooling from Rocky Mount to Bassett, VA to volunteer at the high school football game. This was a benefit game to be played at Bassett High School in northern Henry County, Virginia. Bassett High School was hosting Floyd County High School. As members of the chain crew, we were assigned to the visiting team sideline, in this case Floyd County.

While I lived in Franklin County, my brother and his wife, Bobby and Pam Clark, lived in Floyd County. Both counties adjoined Henry County – Franklin County to the north and Floyd County to the west. On the night of August 21, both my brother and I had traveled to the small town of Bassett for different reasons. I was there to work the football game. My brother and his wife had traveled to Bassett to attend a church service at T.R.A.S.H. Ministry – a biker church.

The location of the church and the football field is not more than two miles apart, as the crow flies. On this evening, two brothers would spend their last night on this earth together with just that distance between them. Neither knew the other was in Bassett that night.

As this was a benefit football game and did not count against the regular season standings, the mood on the sideline was much lighter. During the course of the game, as part of the chain crew, I worked the Floyd County sideline. I would throw out the occasional comment about my brother to an unsuspecting member of the Floyd County staff. Every once in a while, a remark about my brother would be returned. Many of them knew him. He had been a part of their community for over twenty years.

The game had reached just about halftime when an ambulance parked at the stadium had to leave. Just a short distance to the west of the stadium, on Rt. 57A (also known as Riverside Drive), another ambulance had developed a mechanical problem, overheated, and caught fire. From the stadium, we could see the column of smoke rising into the sky. We could hear the oxygen cylinders, contained within the ambulance, exploding in the incredible heat of the fire. The smoke was thick and black. It seemed to rise in a column a hundred feet into the air. After a brief time, the smoke column changed from black to gray indicative of the fire crews getting the fire under control and eventually extinguishing it. In all truthfulness, while all of this was going on, we were not certain as to what was burning. It was only later that we found out it was an ambulance.

The game continued to its scheduled completion. Billy and I headed to our car and the drive home. Our route of travel was eastbound on 57A to Rt. 220 north. We exited Bassett High School in a direction opposite of where the ambulance burned. As my friend and I talked and traveled northbound on Rt. 220, I nearly passed a state trooper in an unmarked car. He suddenly pulled into a parking lot at a convenience store. I suspected that he may have done so just to allow me to pass him so that he could pull me over. That did not happen. I only mention it here, as it is peculiar to me the things that we remember.

I dropped my friend off at our meeting point and headed to the local McDonald's. I was hungry for a bite to eat and my wife would often like an ice cream treat or pie. As I arrived home and backed into my driveway, I noticed the clock on my dashboard read 10:06 p.m.

At approximately 1:30 a.m., our home telephone rang. It is often said that not much good happens after midnight. On the other end of the telephone line was a voice of devastation. It was my 78-year-old mother, Nancy. She was calling to tell me that my brother and sister-in-law had been killed in a motorcycle accident. "Bobby and Pam are no longer with us," she said. There was such pain and anguish in her voice. We didn't talk long. My sister was with her at the time.

I was crushed. I didn't want to believe it. A feeling of devastation came over me. And, just as quickly, a peace hit me. I didn't understand it. But I was able to lay back down and quickly fell asleep. It seemed as though I was awake for only a few minutes.

Later Saturday morning, I awakened early trying to process what had happened only a few hours before. I began to learn about some details of the accident. It happened in Bassett, Virginia. There had been an ambulance fire; a road closure; a detour. Suddenly it hit me again. I had spent the entire evening just a mile or so away from my brother. Neither of us knew it. I had spent the evening in sight of where the accident would occur. I had known about the fire. The time the accident was reported to have occurred – 10:06 p.m. This was the moment that I was backing into my driveway in Boones Mill. Suddenly, the sense of devastation passed over me again. And, in a breath, a peace enveloped me. A peace that I had only experienced a time or two before in my life. A peace that was calming, reassuring, and comforting overcame me. A peace that I would later learn was written of in the Bible, *Philippians 4:7 (KJV)*, "And the peace of God which passeth all understanding, shall keep your hearts and minds through Christ Jesus."

I began to think of our daughters. All three of them were living away from home. The idea of giving them such news over the telephone was too much to bear. I also did not want them learning of the news over social media. I knew that I would have to tell one of them over the phone – our youngest, Whitney. She was volunteering with some friends at a river house in Maryland for an inner city church youth retreat.

I decided to travel first to Liberty University in Lynchburg, Virginia, where Caitlin was attending college. She was serving as a Resident Adviser. She was surrounded by several friends when I arrived. As I explained to her what had happened (or at least what I knew as of that time), tears flowed down her face. I was able to hold her and comfort her as she adjusted to the news. We prayed together and spent a little time together.

Next, it came time to notify our youngest, Whitney. I texted Whitney and asked if she could have whoever was in charge that weekend give me a call. When he called me, I explained that I had devastating news to deliver to Whitney and I did not want her to be alone after I gave her the news. He arranged for Whitney to come to the phone while he and some of the other volunteers rallied around her. It was a difficult thing to do.

Before leaving Lynchburg, I sat in the parking lot outside of my daughter's dorm building and telephoned a mutual friend of mine and my brother, Neal Turner. Neal serves as a pastor and a local emergency manager. Mine and Bobby's paths crossed with Neal in the course of our work. Neal shared additional details about the accident that he had learned. Neal was hesitant to relate the details to me. But I needed to hear the information. And I appreciated the manner in which Neal was talking with me. That day, Neal transitioned from being a mutual friend, to being my brother. I love Neal Turner.

As I made my drive back to Roanoke, Virginia, I intended to catch up with our eldest daughter, Jordan, as she was leaving work. I did not see the sense in upsetting her at the beginning of her work shift. Unfortunately, news of the accident broke on social media before I reached my destination. Jordan telephoned me to ask if the reports of her aunt and uncle's accident were true. She had learned of the accident before I could tell her.

Between the phone calls and the personal conversations, my mind bounced around the idea of what I might say if I was asked to speak at their funeral. Plans for the funeral were not even in the works yet, and still, my mind raced around different ideas.

Bobby was born to Bob and Nancy Clark in 1956. He was the eldest of six children. Pam was the youngest of two children and was born in 1959. Her parents, Lewis and Christine Judd, had lived in Amissville, Virginia. Bobby and Pam were united in marriage at Amissville United Methodist Church on Saturday, June 19, 1976. They lived for more than 39 years on this earth as a couple, nearly twice as long as they lived on this earth as individuals.

To look at them and spend time with them, one could walk away thinking they were nearly perfect people. But there was at least one flaw. They both cheered for the Dallas Cowboys.

Bobby and Pam lived lives of service to others. This was evidenced, in part, by the vocations they chose. Bobby began his career as a firefighter with the Fairfax County Fire Department. He later attained a certification as a Cardiac Technician (a precursor to paramedic). He was promoted to the rank of Sergeant. He spent significant time on assignments at Station 17 (Centreville) and Station 1 (McLean). An on-the-job back injury would cut his firefighting career short. It did not deter him in his service to others.

Pam became a nurse after high school. She started her nursing career at an orthopedic practice located on the north side of Warrenton. She continued her nursing career working in hospital surgery departments, home care, and hospice.

Bobby and Pam also volunteered with local fire and EMS agencies. They gave of themselves with volunteer departments in Amissville and Warrenton.

Chapter 1: *A Journey Begins*

Bobby and Pam were parents to two children, Robin and Torrey.

Bobby was able to return to work following his on-the-job injury as an employee of the Virginia Department of Emergency Services, later to be called the Virginia Department of Emergency Management. They would move from Northern Virginia to Richmond where Bobby accepted a role as a Resource Officer working out of the central office. Later, he would be offered a position as a Hazardous Materials Response Officer. Their family would relocate to Southwest Virginia living first in Pulaski County and then settling in Floyd. Pam would continue her nursing career at Radford Hospital, later renamed Carilion New River Valley Medical Center.

During their time these first six to seven years, Bobby would establish many relationships with folks in the emergency management, EMS, fire service, and hazardous materials communities across Virginia. His faith in his Lord and Savior, Jesus Christ, would also deepen. Their family attended Abundant Life Church in Pilot, VA. His pastor was Larry Meador. Bobby would complete studies and develop spiritually, eventually being named as an Associate Pastor of the church. Along the way, a friendship with another pastor, Dan Whitlock, would take root.

Bobby would leave the Virginia Department of Emergency Management to accept an assignment as a missionary in a remote Chinese village. Pam and their son, Torrey, would join him in missionary service. They were assigned to a village that was so remote, there was not a written language amongst the people. Bobby would joke that the children of the village would call him Michael Jordan. They were in this village to serve God's people.

After two years, they returned to Southwest Virginia where Bobby completed his career working as the local emergency manager in Pulaski and then Floyd Counties.

"Fear thou not; for I am with thee: be not dismayed; for I am thy God: I will strengthen thee; yea, I will help thee; yea, I will uphold thee with the right hand of my righteousness."
Isaiah 41:10 (KJV)

CHAPTER 2

THE ACCIDENT

PSALM 116:15 (KJV)

"Precious in the sight of the LORD is the death of his saints."

The night of the accident, Bobby and Pam had traveled from Floyd to Bassett to attend a church known as T.R.A.S.H. Ministry. T.R.A.S.H. stands for *Totally Redeemed Anointed Servants of the Most High*. For the context of this story, I refer to it as a "biker church." That same night, I had traveled from Boones Mill to Bassett to volunteer at a high school football game.

While Bobby and Pam attended church, I was at the local high school volunteering at the high school football game. An ambulance had caught fire and burned just a short distance away from the football stadium.

By the time the football game ended, the ambulance fire had been extinguished. The road (57A), west of the football stadium, remained closed while emergency crews completed their investigation and cleaned the fire scene. This resulted in a portion of the road being closed and a detour being set up.

A man named C.J. Martin had been at the high school stadium that night as well. His son, Cornel Martin, performed with the Bassett High School Marching Band. Because of Cornel's involvement with the band, they ended up leaving the stadium later than I did. I lived in the opposite direction from the scene of this accident. I made a right turn out of the stadium parking lot, headed to Rt. 220 north to travel home.

C.J. and his son needed to travel west on 57A to reach their home. When they reached the scene of the ambulance fire, they were detoured behind a CVS and directed to take T.B. Stanley Highway over to Rt. 57 to complete their journey home. As they traveled along the detour and reached T.B. Stanley Highway, a left turn was necessary.

At the same time, Bobby and Pam, riding the lead motorcycle, traveled from Rt. 57 down T.B. Stanley Highway toward 57A. They intended to take 57A home to Floyd, Virginia.

When C.J. made the left-hand turn onto T.B. Stanley Highway, he accidentally turned into the wrong travel lane (to the left of the double-yellow lines). His truck and Bobby and Pam's motorcycle were approximately 250 feet apart and on a collision course. Witnesses reported that both vehicles took evasive maneuvers. The handlebars of the motorcycle were quickly pulled hard to the right and the motorcycle slid safely away from the truck, never making contact. But Bobby and Pam were thrown to the asphalt. Their bodies were thrown into the path of the truck. The front tires rolled over their bodies, killing them both instantly.

Pastor Dan Whitlock and his wife Sabrina, who had traveled from Floyd to Bassett with Bobby and Pam were on the motorcycle directly behind them. He came to an abrupt stop and abandoned his bike. Sprinting to the front of the truck, he tried to lift the front wheels off of their bodies. He tried to pull the bodies from beneath the truck – to no avail. C.J. and his son were devastated by what had happened. It was a horrible accident that resulted in the loss of two lives.

Word quickly traveled back to the biker church, T.R.A.S.H. Ministry. They heard there was an accident involving someone from their church. The pastor, Mike Price, shared that when the news arrived, they were charged up with some emotion. They wanted to know who was involved, how bad it was, and if there was anything they could do. Pastor Price likes to say, "We are not motorcycle enthusiasts. We are bikers – long hair, tattoo-covered, leather vest-wearing, bible-carrying, Jesus-loving bikers." A group of them charged out of the church parking lot to race over to T.B. Stanley Highway (about a mile away).

An interesting point to note is that Mike Price had trained as a junior pastor under my brother Bobby, once upon a time. Mike has shared with me that Bobby was there the night that Mike began his relationship with

Jesus Christ. They knew each other well.

When they arrived, they approached the other bikers that had been traveling with Bobby and Pam. Quickly, they learned who was involved. They also discovered that Bobby and Pam had already arrived in heaven with Our Father. There was nothing that could be done for them. They turned their attention to the driver of the truck and his son. C.J. and his son happened to be black. This group of bikers walked up T.B. Stanley Highway to where the man and his son were located. C.J.'s wife, Fernanda Martin, later stated that when they saw this group walking toward them, they were gripped with fear. They did not know what was about to happen.

Consider all that was going on in our society in 2015. The civil unrest that was occurring in places like Ferguson, Missouri (2014) and Baltimore, Maryland (2015). Now, get this image in your mind for just a minute. On a rural stretch of roadway in southwest Virginia, a black man is involved in a fatal accident with two people on a motorcycle, and two dozen bikers roll up onto the scene on a Friday night. Think of all that is going on in our world. Let that image sink in for just a moment. Imagine the emotions that must have been surging.

As the bikers reached them, they encircled C.J. and his son, laid hands on them, and began to pray for them. They prayed that the son would not be harmed by what he experienced. And they prayed that the driver of the truck would be lifted and protected from his involvement in the accident.

One of the EMS providers who had responded to render care to Bobby and Pam observed what was taking place between the bikers and the two people from the truck. There was nothing that he could do to help Bobby and Pam. He approached the pastor of the biker church. He put his finger into the pastor's chest and stated, "I want to know the God you serve." He accepted Jesus Christ as his Savior right there on the side of T.B. Stanley Highway – right in the midst of all that had happened.

"It is evidence of lives lived well when you are positively impacting others, even through your passing." I am here to tell you that Bobby and Pam lived well.

Bobby and Pam's lifeless bodies were transported to Memorial Hospital of Martinsville and Henry County. They were not done giving of themselves yet. Bobby was a registered organ donor. Pam was not. Their daughter, Robin, was contacted and asked about Pam's organs. She had to endure an extensive process to allow Pam's organs to be donated also. More than ten people were helped with the viable organs that Bobby and Pam were able to donate.

On Sunday, less than 48 hours after the accident. Robin, and her husband Greg Quesinberry, telephoned the Martin family. Among other things, they wanted to let C.J. Martin and his family know that they understood this was a terrible accident. Robin wanted to ensure that they knew we as a family were going to move on a path of forgiveness. She wanted C.J. to know that she forgave him. She wanted him to know that she loved him. This move of forgiveness did not take place months later or weeks later. This happened within hours of her losing both parents.

C.J. would later share that the telephone call from Robin enabled him to make it to the next day. That act of love and mercy on her part, poured life and hope into him. He would later reflect that Bobby and Pam's daughter telephoned him to express love and forgiveness without ever seeing, meeting, or knowing who he was.

In the days that followed, Robin's actions regarding C.J.'s situation continued. As news reports began to post on social media outlets, people began to post comments in response. Many of the comments expressed condolences to our family for our loss; however, some were messages about what should happen to the driver of the truck. To say that these specific messages were vile and ugly would be an understatement. Robin and my sister Susan, immediately posted messages to counter these. Robin specifically retorted, "You don't know this man. I do. You do not know the situation." She pleaded for people to stop posting such messages and to pray for ALL involved. Her response elicited some apologies. That is a rarity on social media these days.

My mother, Nancy, lives in Culpeper, Virginia. She was not going to be traveling to Southwest Virginia for the visitation and funeral until Thursday, August 27th, 2015. Many of my family live in close proximity to her and were checking in on her and looking after her. I was calling her every day to let her know I was thinking about her.

On Monday afternoon, I telephoned her. My sister answered the phone. She told me, "It's not a good day." I explained that I understood. I asked her to let mom know that I called, I would call again on Tuesday, and if mom wanted she could call me later.

About 10:00 pm on Monday, my mom called. In a broken, course voice, she asked me if my sister had told me. I replied, "No ma. She just said it wasn't a good day." My mom said, "I got a letter from your brother today." My brother, who was killed in a motorcycle accident on Friday night had hand-written a letter to my mom on Friday morning. He wrote to tell her how much he loved her, how good a mom she was to us six kids. He apologized for not coming to visit her more often; and he told her how much he was looking forward to coming up for her birthday in September. He wanted to sit on her front porch, sip on some coffee, tell stories, and enjoy one another's company. When she finished describing the letter to me she became quiet. I replied in a whisper, "What a treasure. What a treasure. His last thoughts were of you. You know exactly how he felt about you."

Reflecting on the letter my brother had written, I considered a difference in the way that Bobby and I lived our lives. You did not part company from Bobby and not hear that you mattered to him. He would let you know that he loved you, that he appreciated you. He was even accomplishing this through letters he would write to people. I realized in a moment that I needed to do better. I realized the fractured existence of many relationships, some of which could be enhanced if I would just speak words of life and love into the lives of others.

"But there is forgiveness with thee, that thou mayest be feared."
Psalm 130:4 (KJV)

CHAPTER 3

THE FUNERAL
AND BURIAL

1 Thessalonians 4:13 (KJV)

"But I would not have you to be ignorant, brethren,
concerning them which are asleep, that ye sorrow not, even as others
which have no hope."

On Wednesday my youngest brother, Sam, telephoned me to let me know that Robin wanted to know if I would deliver the eulogy on behalf of the family. This was something I wanted to do. But frankly, I did not have a solid relationship with everyone in my family. I was somewhat surprised, but appreciative that I was asked. Within moments of accepting this assignment, I became apprehensive. I had been thinking since Saturday (the day after the accident) what I might say if given the opportunity. But that was hypothetical. When it was confirmed that I would speak, the hypothetical became a reality. I spent time in prayer. I talked with my wife, my daughters, and others in my family about exactly what I would consider saying.

Thursday was the day of the visitation. It promised to be emotional for several reasons. Bobby and Pam were going to be buried with full fire department honors. I was suddenly going to be in the midst of so many people, something that I had not relished in the past. My youngest brother, Sam, had put together the video montage of Bobby and Pam's life. Norman, my other younger brother, had helped arrange for all of the fire department involvement. My sister, Susan, was charged with getting my mom to Southwest Virginia and to be her escort for the visitation and funeral. I saw it as my role to help put folks at ease. Both the people who were coming for the visitation/funeral and the family who were going through a traumatic time.

I estimated 1,200 to 1,500 people attended the visitation. I had positioned myself toward the end of the receiving line, close to the exit from the parlor. As people entered the parlor room at the opposite end, I observed countless people almost come to a sudden stop, catch their breath, and even place a hand over their chest as they saw me. Bobby and I looked enough alike that it caught some folks by surprise. More than one person told me as they came through the receiving line, that they thought for a split second that I was Bobby.

On Friday morning, the family gathered at the church in Pilot, Virginia for the funeral service. My two younger brothers and I would serve as pallbearers along with seven other men. It had been arranged that Bobby and Pam would be buried together in the same casket. I did not even know you could do that. It was a closed casket service. Bobby had been placed on his back and his wife of 39 years was placed on her side. Bobby's arm was wrapped around her and their hands were clasped together. It took ten of us to carry the casket.

Five speakers had been scheduled for the funeral. A senior pastor and his wife from Mt. Zion Christian Church, a man who serves as a pastor and captain of Slate Mountain Presbyterian Church and the Floyd County Sheriff's Office, and a former pastor from Abundant Life Fellowship Church would join me as the speakers during the funeral. I was nervous. I wondered if I would hold up well enough to deliver the remarks. How would folks, particularly my family, receive my remarks. Would I be "religious" enough?

The service began with a reading of a poem by Kim McNeil, who was also the author of the poem. As I would learn, Bobby and Pam visited the McNeil's church the Sunday following the mass shooting in Charleston, S.C. at the historic Emanuel African Methodist Episcopal Church just two months prior to their deaths. They had visited the McNeil's church as an expression of their love and unity. They saw the attack in Charleston as an attack on all Christians. They saw it as an attack on our unity as a Christian faith. They wanted to stand in solidarity with the McNeil's and their church family. With permission of Kim McNeil, I have included this poem here.

The Mission of a Missionary by Lady Kim McNeil
Mt. Zion Christian Church, Floyd, VA

From the first day that we met,
Our spirits connected as we prayed in the vestibule.
For we all knew on that day,
That UNITY and PRAYER were our most powerful tools.

We prayed for one another...
And for the whole world to come together as one.
For they had a divine mission as missionaries...
To lead everyone to God's Holy and Precious Son.

They saw no shade or color of people's skin...
Their hearts were Godly pure.
They were fulfilling their mission as missionaries
On that you can be sure.

Bobby and Pam certainly touched our lives
In what seems way too short a time.
They have shown us the heart of a missionary,
And this loss seems to have no reason or rhyme.

But we know the steps of the righteous are ordered by the Lord,

And God's word is simply true.
They have been a great witness to the real mission of a missionary
And they showed everyone they met just what we ALL should do.

The enemy would have us to focus on how they left us…
But God says, "Celebrate their life…how humble and
faithful they were to always give!!!"
For they knew the greatest mission of a missionary…
To spread the Gospel in kindness that people may eternally live.

Our thoughts and prayers are with you,
As you face uncertain days.
May the Lord watch over you, comfort, and keep you.
And may your family UNIFY in all your ways.

May the peace of God be with you and always remember…
It's not how you start your journey, what happens or how long it lasts.
But how you finish, and Bobby and Pam finished STRONG.
May God Bless you ALL!!!

With Unconditional Love…Lady Kim McNeil

I wanted to reflect positively upon the lives of Bobby and Pam. I also wanted to inject humor into the service. I wanted to make people laugh. I already expected there to be tears of sadness. I stood to deliver the eulogy. Immediately, I went off script. I spoke as I felt led. In the very beginning, my voice broke and I thought it was over. My father-in-law would later comment that he nearly left his seat to come stand by me for comfort and strength. Then suddenly, I composed myself and delivered the eulogy just as I had planned.

During the course of the eulogy, I heard outbursts of laughter. I saw my mom smile. (Which was a specific intention of one of my comments.) I witnessed tears flow. I knew I had struck the right balance. People applauded at the conclusion of my remarks. They were expressing their appreciation for the representation of the lives of Bobby and Pam that I had shared. Below, I have provided the transcript of the eulogy I shared that day. A friend, Keith Dowler, unobtrusively used his iPhone to create an audio file of my spoken remarks.

The Eulogy

"And now abideth faith, hope, charity, these three; but the greatest of these is charity." 1 Corinthians 13:13 (KJV)

"So as I sit and listen this morning, I realize once again all glory to God. As I thought through this week what I might say today on behalf of the family, the very words that these people who already spoke were spoken through me to the words on these pages. It is just so fulfilling and rewarding to talk (about my brother and his wife)."

"I titled my words, 'Faith. Hope. And Love. A Celebration of Life.'

"Good morning to everyone. Wow! This is awesome to see. On behalf of the family, I would like to thank each of you for being here today. As evidenced by the turnout last night and again today, Bobby and Pam certainly impacted a great number of people. And this is but a tiny fraction of the people that we know they touched. They made a difference!

"Before I continue, I would like to follow Robin's example and ask that each of you continue to extend prayers to Mr. C.J. Martin and his family. He and his family are experiencing their own pain and heartache. They need God's love and comfort every bit as much as those of us grieving our loss.

"To those of you that do not know me, I am J.T. Clark. Or as I always liked to say, I am Bobby Clark's younger brother. Being at the funeral home last night, I had more than one person stop me and say, 'When I walked in here, my heart skipped a beat because I looked over in the corner.' I started to get the buzz cut and kind of finish off the picture there.

"My goal in speaking with you today is to help us along in the grieving process and frankly this is doing as much for me as it is for anybody else. But just as importantly, I am here to share in the celebration of the lives of Bobby and Pam. It is my hope that over the next several minutes that some of us will cry; but that you also might laugh. But most importantly, my hope that the words that I share with you will give us all moments for reflection. I think you can already tell, but I'll forewarn you anyway, that I'm probably going to be crying and laughing right along with you. So, make sure I'm not the only one. Let's go for this little ride together.

"As I thought over this past week what I might say, I quickly realized that Bobby and Pam sure did give us a lot of material to work with. Holy crow!

There are volumes upon volumes of life experiences and memories that I could share with you. And the great thing about their lives is that each of you have your own volumes and volumes of material. Because that's how they lived. As Teddy Atkins, a Battalion Chief with the City of Roanoke recently said, there are givers and takers in this world, and Bobby and Pam were givers. They both gave us all so much. And again, we have those materials and memories from which to reflect. What a treasure! What a treasure.

"All of the men in our family certainly married up. This started with our father. No disrespect to my dad, but all of you who know of our mother, certainly understand this. Well, Bobby also married out of his league. What Pam saw in Bobby was a headscratcher for those that grew up with him. Of course, that could be said for the rest of us Clark boys as well. Am I right? In reflecting on our individual marriages, one constant was Bobby had a significant role in all of our weddings. He served as a best man; he was a groomsman; he officiated; even with our sister he stepped in place of our father and walked her down the aisle. And our parents, my goodness, five boys and a girl. They were tested early and often. But to say that our mother was a tad bit naïve would be an understatement.

"For a while, it was routine for our mother to take Bobby and her niece, Cathy, back-to-school shopping. This trip usually culminated with a meal and a visit to the theater. Our mother was so sheltered that when she took Bobby and Cathy to see the movie 'The Godfather,' it wasn't until the scene where the horse's head ended up in the bed, that she realized that this was not a religious movie.

"Bobby was larger than life, but Pam made Bobby a better man. Bobby was twenty years old when he got married. And Pam was eighteen. They were married for more than thirty-nine years. They spent twice the amount of time on this earth as a married couple than they did as individuals. To your point, their marriage was a living example of what is meant by the biblical definition. They embraced the traditional wedding vows. They became one. You could hardly refer to one or the other. It was always, 'Bobby and Pam;' 'Bobby and Pam.' And as we heard the others speak this morning, it was 'Bobby and Pam.'

"They routinely made the choice to love one another. They made this choice in sickness and in health; for richer and for poorer. They humbled themselves before God to allow His love, His grace, and His mercy to flow through them. They were selfless in their love for one another.

"Of course, at different times in their lives they certainly experienced their

own share of pain. And while these times were difficult to bear, the fact that they had one another and their faith in God helped them endure. I think the physical pain that they suffered was made even more so when it impacted or tempered their ability to be of service to others. So, it wasn't as much that they were hurting, but that they were at times limited to what or how they could help somebody else.

"I said in my introduction that they left me much material with which to work. I certainly had to cull the list to a few specific examples. And as I reflected on some of the stories, I realized that Bobby probably came along at a good time in that social media was not invented in his youth. Let me add here that if anyone would like to share a story of Bobby or Pam or Bobby and Pam in the days, months, and years ahead, look up any of us, because we would love to listen – Sammy, Norman, my mother, Susan, Robin, Torrey, our brother Howard.

"If you come talk to us about some of the stories, these are some of the topics that you might get to hear about:

- Becoming an Eagle Scout, as Bobby was;

- Or, you might hear a story about eating bowls of steamed, spiced shrimp with the tail and shell still on;

- We could also talk about manual transmissions;

- Or, an evening at Frost Diner;

- You have to have a few years on you to understand this next one, but you might even also ask about streaking;

- Bobby enjoyed NASCAR;

- We loved the Buckeyes, I know they are coming to town in a few days; and

- The only bone I ever had to pick with Pam is she converted Bobby. He was raised a die-hard Redskin fan. And on June 19, 1976, he converted. . . to become a Cowboys fan. I could never go to a game with him; I just couldn't do it.

- Bobby, Pam, and I ran on the Thursday Night crew with the Warrenton Volunteer Rescue Squad and the stories there are endless;

- We could talk to you about Christmas Caroling; Sumo Wrestling; joyriding; and many, many, many more stories.

"I said the title of my paper was 'Faith. Hope. And Love,' so let's talk about the Faith part for just a minute. Bobby and Pam had a deep and abiding faith. They were open and willing to share this with others. Long before he was ordained, for they served as missionaries, they were a living testimony. 'Service to others, not self' was a code they lived by. This was evidenced by the relationships they cultivated and the vocations they pursued. A strong demonstration of their faith was shared with me very early in their marriage.

"I was riding in their car with them on (Rt.) 613 up in Amissville; not quite a teenager. I was in the backseat. We were driving up the road and they knew I was at a time in my life when I was really trying to understand the idea of having a deep and meaningful, personal relationship with Christ. I remember telling them that I was confused about some of the things that I had been taught about God. And Bobby asked me, 'Do you know where you will spend eternity?' And of course, I replied, 'Yeah; I know where I will be.' He challenged me as to how I knew. I replied that I knew because I am a nice guy. I do good things. Then he asked me how long I thought that eternity lasted. I was barely a teenager. How long is eternity? Eternity is forever. He pushed back, and he wanted to know if I really knew what that meant. And he went on to give me this description of eternity that stuck with me and crystalized my view of this.

"His story went something like this: Take every grain of sand that exists here on planet earth and pile it up on the east coast of North America. Then take a single seagull and have that single seagull pick up a single grain of sand and fly it to Europe and drop it on the coast over there. And that seagull comes back and continues until every grain of sand has (been) transported across the Atlantic and dropped in Europe. And once that's completed, the same seagull picks up a grain of sand and comes back to the east coast of North America. Bobby went on to say that this amount of time to accomplish this represents the very first days of eternity. Bobby and Pam went on to inform me that the only way I could ensure where I ended up for eternity was through a personal relationship with our Savior, Jesus.

"Hope was demonstrated – they were filled with hope, Bobby and Pam. Just like their faith and love, they were willing to share their hope with any that sought it. In fact, sometimes you got a dose of it even when you didn't know you needed it. A beautiful aspect of their hope was that they literally and figuratively met you wherever you were. If you were experiencing a joyous occasion, they celebrated with you. They were not jealous and did not covet your circumstance. They were just happy that it was yours.

"Bobby and Pam never met a stranger. Everyone was always welcome, and they were ready to help anyone. If it was a time when you were in a valley and were experiencing a painful situation of your own, they hurt with you. In fact, in one of the scriptures that was read to you was, 'Jesus wept.' When you were hurting, Bobby and Pam hurt with you. They didn't know the reason that you had to have the experience; they just knew something good was going to come from it. They shared in the pain even if they were experiencing their own valley at the time. And just as they were not jealous in your good times, neither were they judgmental when you were having a difficult time. They were just there. They were present. They were with you. They were with me.

"When it comes to love, there was no question that you knew where you stood with the two of them. Somebody, last night, reflected this statement to me, 'They never left any doubt that they loved and appreciated the people in their lives.' There was a teacher that came up to me, last night, and said that Bobby routinely went to the grandchildren's school and had lunch with them. And he would stay through the entire lunch cycle as all of the grandchildren rotated through. He would make it a point to approach each teacher and thank her for the service she provided in the school. And that's the way Bobby and Pam were. They wanted you to know that they valued and appreciated others. They always told the people around them this.

"Oh boy the days that their daughter, Robin, and their son, Torrey, were born were among the happiest days of their lives. They were overjoyed and wanted to share the experience. They also rejoiced in the arrival of their grandchildren. They loved their children and grandchildren unconditionally. They cherished the time they got to spend with them on the farm, at sporting events, at the school, and on and on and on.

"I will close with this story which is the best evidence I can offer about their expression of love. On Monday, August 24th, our mother received a letter in the mail. This was a letter written by Bobby on August 21st, the day he and Pam would be called home. In the letter, he expressed his love for his mother. He spoke of how he and Pam were looking forward to being with her for a few days in September. Nothing fancy. Just looking forward to sitting on the porch, sipping coffee, and telling stories. He reminded her of how strong of a woman she is. And how great of a mother she is. (He got that right). He shared some Bible verses with her. And he told her he loved her. In the end, he left no doubt about his love for the people in his life.

"My question for all of us is, 'Do the people in our lives know how we feel about them?' I know I have some work to do to be a better reflection of their example of God's love for us. As Alan Jackson sings, 'Faith. Hope. And Love. are some good

things He gave us. The greatest is love.'

"*God bless you all and Godspeed.*"

Pastor Larry Meador was the final speaker for the service. Through his remarks, I learned that the letter my mom received three days after the accident was not the only letter my brother wrote that morning. He wrote another letter. This letter was mailed to Torrey, their son, who was incarcerated at the time of the accident. In this letter, he wrote to Torrey wishing that he could live a life more like the life Stephen lived as referenced in the Book of Acts, Chapter 7.

Stephen was martyred for the life he lived for Christ and his desire to draw ever closer. As he was stoned to death, he proclaimed his faith and called on God to show mercy on the ones who were killing him. This was the essence of the letter my brother wrote to his son on the very day he was killed.

The Processional

The processional from the church to the cemetery was a long one. There were 500 people in attendance and many were planning to make the trip. The processional was led by fire apparatus from the area. Members of a chapter of the Red Knights International Firefighters Motorcycle Club also served as escorts for the hearse.

Upon arrival at the cemetery, we could see the aerial ladders of two ladder trucks from neighboring jurisdictions. The ladder trucks had been positioned in a fashion that would allow a United States flag to be draped down from the apex of the ladders. The processional would drive between these two stationary ladder trucks and directly beneath the flag. A burial plot located on a small knoll near a cherry tree was selected.

Bobby and Pam were laid to rest with fire department and nursing honors, respectively. Elements of the graveside service were included to highlight their dedication to serving others. A firefighter's poem and a nurse's poem were each read aloud. The casket was draped with a United States flag that was folded by a fire department honor guard and presented to the family. Near the conclusion of the service, Floyd County Emergency Services honored my brother by dispatching his final call.

In many jurisdictions and localities, fire departments and other first response organizations choose to honor in this manner those who have died. In the case of my brother, the Floyd County 911 Center attempted to reach my brother through his Fairfax County badge number. They called for his badge number three times. When he did not respond, they announced his final call. A transcript of this radio communication follows. The transcript was taken from a digital recording that was provided to me by the Floyd County 911 Center. The call was announced by dispatcher Shawn Conner.

The Final Call

August 28, 2015 @ 13:32 hours

"Floyd County to Fairfax County Badge Number 423. (Pause) Floyd County to Fairfax County Badge Number 423. (Pause) Floyd County to Fairfax County Badge Number 423. (Pause)"

"Attention all units and stations for Floyd County. It is with deep regret that we announce the passing of retired Fairfax County Fire Department Sergeant and retired Floyd County ES1, Bobby Clark. The tones have been dropped for his last alarm. May the sun shine upon his path. May the wind always be at his back. And may the Lord hold him in the palm of His hand, until we meet again. Floyd County clear. 13:32."

The Roadside Vigil

The evening of the funeral, the folks from the biker church, led by their pastor, decided to return to the scene of the accident. They returned to hold a vigil. They wanted to place two roadside markers in remembrance of Bobby and Pam. They went back to the scene of the accident to pray. They did not return alone.

I have not shared a couple of details with you until now. C.J. Martin is also a pastor. His church, House of Purpose Ministries, is located at a storefront in a shopping plaza right off of Route 57A (Riverside Drive). From the front door of his church, you can practically see the football stadium where we had been that night; the site of the ambulance fire; and the location of the fatal accident. You could practically wrap your arms around the entirety of the situation that unfolded the night of the accident.

On this evening, the people of T.R.A.S.H. Ministry gathered along T.B. Stanley Highway with the people of House of Purpose Ministries. The state trooper who investigated the accident was so moved by what took place the night of the wreck, he also attended the vigil.

I am going to ask you to stop and reflect on this just a moment. Once again, when you think of all that is going on in our world, the division, the anger and hatred; consider this gathering along a small stretch of roadway in rural, Southwest Virginia. A group of men and women of different backgrounds, races, cultures, and vocations coming together to express love and life. They had come together to lift those who were hurting. Powerful!

The people from these churches and this community gathered. They came together to pray for the Clark family. They came together to pray for the Martin family. And they prayed for the Martin's church family. They prayed for his ministry. They prayed for our community. But it didn't stop with prayer. The folks from the biker church gave money and prepared food for the Martin family. They wanted to help sustain the Martin family in the days and weeks after the accident.

Through the pain and anguish that C.J. Martin was experiencing, Pastor Mike Price encouraged him to speak. Pastor Price told him that the people at the vigil needed to hear from him. BTW21, a local cable origination channel, was on the scene to record and report on some of the activity of the vigil. It was yet another step in the healing process for all concerned.

The Healing Process Continues

One week after the funeral (two weeks after the fatal accident), C.J. Martin, his wife and a couple of leaders from his church, made the trip from Bassett, Virginia to Floyd, Virginia to meet with Robin Quesinberry and members of her immediate family. They wanted to visit with them so that the healing process could continue.

The ride to cover that distance is some 40 miles by automobile. The road is a winding mountain road. I cannot imagine what would have been going through the minds of those making the trip.

On June 10, 2016, C.J. Martin and I were traveling together to visit Robin's brother Torrey, who was incarcerated at the New River Valley Regional Jail. On our ride home from that visit, C.J. shared a couple of details with me. He reminded me of the example that Bobby and Pam must have been in Robin and Torrey's lives. He described the drive to visit Robin that night, two weeks after the accident. He said, "When we arrived at their home, we pulled up into the driveway. We weren't certain we were at the right place. Jacoby (Stanley), one of the deacons at our church got out of the vehicle to knock on the door. When Robin swung the door open, she brushed past Jacoby and sprinted to the car that I was in. When I got out of the car, she threw her arms around my neck and said, 'I love you.'"

C.J. expressed how powerful it was to have arrived at Robin's home that night and to have been received in such a way. In the natural realm, it is almost incomprehensible. It did a great deal to further cement the healing that was so desperately needed.

"And this is the promise that he hath promised us, even eternal life."
1 John 2:25 (KJV)

CHAPTER 4

MR. MARTIN GOES TO COURT

Ecclesiastes 8:5 (KJV)

"Whoso keepeth the commandment shall feel no evil thing:
and a wise man's heart discerneth both time and judgment"

C.J. Martin was charged in the accident. Society said that he needed to be held accountable for his role in the accident. He was scheduled to go to court on Monday, October 26, 2015 at 2:00 pm. His case would be heard in Henry County General District Court.

About five days before Mr. Martin's hearing, I had something stirring inside me that was causing me to feel like I needed to be there. I did not want to go. Our family was moving on a path of forgiveness. I was afraid if I showed up in the courtroom that I would not be able to hold it together. I was concerned that if I broke down in the courtroom, the judge might make the outcome worse for Mr. Martin. Still, this stirring continued. I wondered if I needed to be in the courtroom to represent Bobby and Pam.

On the day of the hearing, I was still resisting the urge to go. In fact, that morning, I drove 25 minutes in the opposite direction to my place of employment. By 9:00 am, I was sitting at my desk getting myself ready for the week. By 10:00 am, the feeling that I needed to be in the courtroom was so strong, I got in my car and headed south.

About 40 minutes into my one-hour drive, I was south of Rocky Mount. I was about halfway between Rocky Mount and the Henry County Courthouse, when a message came across my spirit. "I need you to pay the fine." I remember saying, "Pay the fine?! This could be thousands of dollars! My wife didn't know where I was going. My family didn't know where I was going. What do you mean you need me to pay the fine?!"

Instantly, I received a second message in response. "You don't worry about a thing. You show up; be ready to pay the fine; and I will make a way."

I have stated previously that my brother was a pastor. I had not been to church in years. This was a life my brother lived. I had not been living the way he had. I did not have a desire to surrender to a Savior. It was not something that I pursued. I arrived at the courthouse about two hours early. I was screened by a Sheriff's Deputy who was stationed at the entrance to the court house. I then proceeded back to the General District Courtroom.

When the opportunity occurred, I made my way inside and grabbed a seat about four rows back from the front on the left-hand side. I sat closer to the center aisle of the courtroom and I was left alone with my thoughts. I reflected on what I had experienced driving to the court house. What did that mean? What was I going to do about it? At the time, my wife and I had been married for 28 years. We did not have a habit of spending thousands of dollars without the other knowing about it. As I sat there I thought, "Okay, I am going to watch this thing play out. Whatever happens, I will go to the clerk and write a check. I will use my drive back to Boones Mill to figure how I will explain this to my wife." Truth-be-known, my wife had already moved in forgiveness as well, and possessed a strong faith. I knew she would understand.

About 40 minutes into my wait, a third message came across my spirit. "I need you to tell the state trooper who you are and why you are here."

What?! Let's reflect for a moment. It was not my idea to come to court that day. I did not want to be there. It was certainly not my idea to pay any fine. And now, I am being asked to stand up, approach three state troopers who were standing in front of the courtroom and tell them what has happened. There is no way. If I do this, they are going to think I am crazy. They are going to want to lock me up.

After finally mustering the courage, I stood up from the wooden bench and walked toward the front of the courtroom. I went to a wall near where the troopers were standing and talking. I stood a few feet away from where they were and eavesdropped on their conversation. I was trying to learn which of the three of them had investigated the accident. When I figured it out, I approached the trio and addressed the trooper in the middle.

"Sir, my name is J.T. Clark. I wasn't subpoenaed to be here. I wasn't invited. I don't have a role. But, I came to pay the fine." The trooper looked back at me as if I was from a different planet. He picked up his investigation folder and he walked me back over to where I had been seated. He sat down on the bench next to me. He leaned into me and said, "Now what did you just tell me?"

I replied, "I came to pay the fine."

His response, "I have been doing this for 37 years, I have not heard anything like this in my entire career." He opened the folder and proceeded to walk me through his investigation. He shared with me the written accident report. He showed me the accident scene photographs. He gave me a narrative explanation of all that occurred that night. He told me, "When I showed this evidence to the Commonwealth's Attorney, he was considering vehicular manslaughter charges against Mr. Martin. In every case I have ever been involved, the family wants more penalty, not less. When he was talking Vehicular Manslaughter, I had not yet discussed it with your family. Something moved within me. I pushed back against the Commonwealth's Attorney and told him not here and not in this case." Mr. Martin was charged with Reckless Driving.

There is a big difference between the seriousness of these two charges. One can be prosecuted as a felony. The other is a major moving traffic violation. One could mean imprisonment and a fine. A guilty verdict in the other case is likely to only carry a fine.

The trooper then goes on to say, "My 24-year-old son was killed in a motor vehicle crash just a couple of years ago. I am still struggling with the circumstances of this. And you come in here and you're going to pay a man's fine." He got up from the bench shaking his head as he walked away.

We still had about 20 minutes before the case would be called. I did not realize it, but the state trooper left the courtroom proper and entered a back area for court officials. I would later discover that he went back there to discuss with the representative from the Commonwealth

Attorney's office what I had told him about paying the fine. The defense attorney was invited to be a part of their discussion.

At 2:00 pm, the judge entered the courtroom and called the case. The attorneys for each side were not yet in the courtroom. A few moments later, the Commonwealth's Attorney's representative entered the courtroom and asked the judge for a few more minutes. She explained that there had been a development. He acquiesced, and she exited the courtroom. In the interim, a couple of other attorneys who were present for other matters made light-hearted comments to the judge about the delay and his penchant for being a rigid time manager. Nearly 15 minutes passed before all parties returned to the courtroom.

As all four individuals approached the judge, I saw who C.J. Martin was for the very first time. He came forward with his attorney, the Commonwealth's Attorney, and the state trooper. Before the judge could utter a word, the state trooper looked over his left shoulder and pointed a finger in my direction stating, "You're a part of this now, too. You better come on up here." I was shaking in my shoes. I got up out of my seat once again and I walked to the area in front of the judge where the others had gathered. I stood to the left of the state trooper. I was positioned at the opposite end of the line from C.J. that had assembled in front of and facing the judge.

The defense attorney spoke and said, "Your Honor, we are prepared to accept a plea deal for Improper Driving." This is about the lowest moving violation charge that could be assessed in such a situation. The judge looked back at the defense attorney as if to say, "Improper driving. I have two dead people here. Someone is going to have to explain something to me." Then, he swore us in and asked the trooper to give an account. The state trooper told the judge the very same story he had told me a short while before. He showed the judge the very same photographs.

When the state trooper wrapped up those details, he told the judge, "Your Honor, there are two more things you need to know." Pointing to his left, he said, "This is J.T. Clark. He is the brother and brother-in-law of the two who were killed." With a slight hesitation he continued, "And, he intends to pay any fine you impose in this case."

When Mr. Martin heard this, he cried out in the courtroom, "Oh my Jesus!" He began to weep openly. What I learned, some seven months later, was that when he entered the courtroom that day, he saw the trooper sitting and talking with me. He told me that when the trooper called for me to come forward, he just knew that I was there as a witness against him. He said, "When I heard what you were really there to do, I just couldn't contain my emotions."

The judge turned his head and looked at me and asked, "What in the world would you do that for?" Now remember, it wasn't my idea to be there. It wasn't my idea to pay the fine. I did not want to talk to the state trooper. I did not want to be standing before the judge. I certainly did not want to speak openly in court. I thought to myself, What in the world have I gotten myself into?

"Well, your Honor. Our family is moving on a path of forgiveness toward Mr. Martin. Frankly, actions speak louder than words. If my being here and paying his fine helps him to accept and receive that forgiveness, to do what he is called to do, enjoy the rest of his life, and enjoy his wife and son...well your honor that's what I am here to do. We love Mr. Martin."

The courtroom was utterly silent. You could have heard the proverbial pin drop in that moment. The judge reached down and picked up a piece of paper. He placed it in front of him. He picked up his ink pen. Practically shaking his head in disbelief, he stated, "A few minutes ago, I was trying to figure out how I could accept a charge of Improper Driving. Now, I am writing on this piece of paper that the fine is $5.00."

I could not believe what I had just heard. I could only think about it for a moment. I quickly reflected on the second message I received in the car on my way to the courtroom, "You don't worry about a thing. You show up. Be ready to pay the fine, and I will make a way." I could not fully comprehend it in the moment.

With the case adjudicated, I walked over to Mr. Martin and we grabbed each other up in a bear hug. As we cried on each other's shoulders, I told him, "I gotcha brother. It's gonna be alright." We held onto each other for minutes. Not a soul dare moved a muscle during this time. The only thing moving were the tears flowing down people's faces.

After we gathered ourselves, C.J. Martin, his wife, his attorney, and I made our way down a corridor to the clerk's office. (I would begin to know Mr. Martin as "C.J.") As we walked, C.J. whispered quietly and said, "You don't have to do this."

I replied, "Oh, yes I do. We are going to take this all the way."

C.J. stopped walking. He grabbed my right hand to shake it. Facing me, he put his other hand on my shoulder. He asked me how my mom was doing. He asked me how my brother's daughter, Robin, was doing. Then, in this moment, C.J. Martin said to me, "Won't you come to my church?" Instinctively, I said yes.

As we proceeded to the clerk's office, I thought to myself, I haven't been to church in years. The first church I am going to go to is a black church, pastored by the man that was driving the truck in my brother's accident.

We arrived at the clerk's office. Keep in mind, the attendant at the window had no idea what had just transpired down a corridor in an adjoining room. In fact, her day consisted of a lot of people not being so happy to be standing in front of her. As we approached, she asked Mr. Martin if he was prepared to pay his entire fine. I withdrew a debit card from my wallet and laid it on the counter and exclaimed to her, "I got this!"

She replied, "There is a 4% fee for paying with a debit card."

I acknowledged that I understood. As the clerk picked up the piece of paper that had been delivered from the courtroom, she reached for a wall phone with her left hand. The state trooper, who had entered the clerk's office from another entrance, asked her, "Is there a problem?"

She replied, "There must be. This piece of paper says the fine is $5.00."

The trooper informed her, "There is no issue. That is the fine."

She totaled up the charges inclusive of the fine, court costs, and the added debit card fee and indicated that just over $68 was owed. The costs were paid, and our group exited into a corridor outside of the courtroom adjacent to the main lobby.

I began to express my concerns and reservations to the defense attorney. I told him that I had hoped that I had not interfered with the process. I was just doing what I was feeling led to do. The defense attorney responded by saying, "You have no idea the impact this had, or will have."

As we continued to talk, the state trooper emerged from the courtroom. He approached our group and informed us that there had been a newspaper reporter in the courtroom for the proceedings. He said the reporter had already spoken with him and was now talking to the Commonwealth's Attorney. He said, "The reporter is going to want to talk to you all next."

Angst overflowed me. I did not want to talk with any reporter. I was not fully certain what had happened. I just knew that I did not want to talk to any reporter. I hurriedly walked down the corridor toward the entrance. As I turned the corner to exit, the Sheriff's Deputy who had screened me when I entered the courtroom came out from behind her desk and said, "I just got a call from someone in the courtroom. I was told to give you a hug before you leave." For just a moment, this woman and I hugged one another. A calmness came over me. I left the building and went straight to my car.

On my ride home, I telephoned my mother. I gave her a quick story about showing up at the court and paying C.J. Martin's fine. When I finished telling her the story, there was silence on the other end of the telephone. I asked my mother, "Ma, did you hear what I said? What do you think?"

She was choked up but she managed to reply, "Son, I am just so proud of you."

I then called my youngest brother and told him what had happened. He was supportive of me, also.

"For if, when we were enemies, we were reconciled to God by the death of his Son, much more, being reconciled, we shall be saved by his life. And not only so, but we also joy in God through our Lord Jesus Christ, by whom we have now received the atonement."
Romans 5:10-11 (KJV)

CHAPTER 5

A STORY IS REPORTED

Hebrews 9:22 (KJV)

*"And almost all things are by the law purged with blood;
and without shedding of blood is no remission."*

Early in the morning of Tuesday, October 27th, I received a text message. It included a link to the *Martinsville Bulletin*. I was asked if I had seen the story that was reported in the newspaper. The headline read, *"Man convicted, fined in fatal crash."* This was the first I had seen of it. I was quite apprehensive about the story. I had not informed all of my family about having gone to court. Having this story reported in a publication that was also available online made me nervous.

I sent the link to my youngest brother. I told him, "Whatever you do, do not share this on social media." To that point, I had not ventured into the online community environment. I neither understood it, nor had a desire to be a part of it.

When my brother read the article, he responded back to me. "I will honor your wishes. But, it isn't going to matter. This story will be shared on Facebook, Twitter, etc. It is going to be out there."

On Wednesday, I was still apprehensive about my involvement. Again, I had not been subpoenaed, nor invited. I was concerned that I had interfered inappropriately with the proceedings in some way. I wanted to offer my apologies to each person involved, but also to thank them for allowing things to happen as they did. When I left Roanoke the morning of the court proceedings, I had no intention of being involved. I did not want to go. I thought I would simply be there to represent my brother. I ended up representing Bobby and Pam in a way that represented their lives – in a way I could have never imagined.

I called the State Police Office where the investigating trooper was assigned. I could not speak with him, but I did speak with the receptionist and the First Sergeant of this office. I also called the Commonwealth's Attorney. The elected official in the office took my call and we talked about what had transpired. He expressed admiration for what had happened and assured me that there was no concern about my involvement. He invited me to speak with the representative from his team who had been in the courtroom that day. He shared that she was new to his office (fresh out of law school, as I understood). When things began to unfold at the courthouse, she had called him for guidance.

When I spoke with her I thanked her for her role in all of it. I thanked her for her willingness to advocate for the process to work out the way it did.

I tried to call the judge. I was informed that I could not speak with him. But if I wanted, I was invited to write him a letter that he may or may not decide to read. I wrote him a letter and put it in the mail.

On Wednesday evening, I was preparing to have dinner with my wife and the telephone rang. The caller ID revealed that the call was from *The Roanoke Times*. As it turns out, *The Roanoke Times* is the sister paper, albeit bigger, to the *Martinsville Bulletin*. I tentatively answered the telephone and the man on the other end informed me that his name was Neil Harvey and that he was in fact a reporter with *The Roanoke Times*. He informed me that he was aware of a story that had appeared in the *Martinsville Bulletin* and wanted to know if I would be willing to be interviewed for a more in-depth story. I expressed my reservations to him. I explained that I had not done what I did for the purposes of publicity. I told him I would need to discuss it with my family before proceeding. He agreed to call me back on Thursday afternoon. If I decided I did not want to participate in an interview, he said he would understand.

After speaking with members of my family, each encouraged me to accept the interview. Each said, "This is a story that needs to be told. This has the potential to impact others."

At 1:00 pm on Thursday, Mr. Harvey telephoned me. He asked if I wanted to be interviewed. With hesitation, I told him yes. What happened next put me at ease. He spent the next 45 minutes asking me about my brother and his wife. He didn't ask about the details of the accident. He didn't ask about the court case. He simply wanted me to share details with him that would introduce them to him, allow him to get to know the two of them. We spoke for nearly two hours. I was hesitant to share with Mr. Harvey how I was moved to go to court. I could not tell him about the "instructions" I received. I could not wrap my head around it myself. I was afraid of what he might think. I was afraid of what would be printed in the newspaper.

He told me he thought an article would appear that weekend. It would not happen. Late Friday evening, he informed me that he still needed more information. He asked if I would talk to him early the next week. He wanted to get some photographs to use in the story, he wanted to interview the state trooper, and speak with C.J. Martin.

On Saturday, I was scheduled to work the NASCAR event at the Martinsville Speedway. It was the fall race. There were two men I was hoping to see during the course of the weekend. The first man was the director of the emergency department of the local hospital. As it turns out, he is also a volunteer with the Bassett Rescue Squad. I approached him to share a perspective that some members of my family had about the accident. You see, the accident occurred around 10:06 pm on Friday night (August 21). The date of Bobby and Pam's deaths was not officially recorded until after midnight on Saturday morning (August 22). Some of my family were concerned that Bobby and Pam might have lingered and suffered as a result. I told this man I did not want him to violate any rules, but it sure would bring comfort to my family if they were assured that Bobby and Pam passed instantly and did not suffer. This man provided me that assurance, which I later shared with my family. He explained that it took a while before their bodies were transported to the hospital following the accident and the date and time recorded by the ER physician reflected the August 22 date.

The second person that I was really hoping to run into was a man named Michael Harrison. I had met Michael at a tabletop exercise our organization had hosted in April 2014. The exercise had involved a simulation of a mass casualty incident occurring at the speedway. Michael led the Raceway Ministry Outreach at the track and participated in the exercise. Michael is also the pastor of The Community Fellowship. I needed to talk to him.

After several visits to the Raceway Ministry Outreach tent located at the speedway, I finally had an encounter with Michael. I asked him if he remembered me. He said that he did. I asked him if he had a few minutes to talk. I needed to tell him what happened. He said he was familiar with the newspaper article that had appeared on Tuesday, then shared more of the details with him. I was still reluctant to talk about the spiritual nature of what I experienced. When I finished, Michael said something to the effect of, "That's a good story, but there is something you need to know. It's not about you."

I was taken aback. I responded, "No. Wait a minute. Didn't you hear what I said?" And I began to go back into the details of it a second time. After listening for a few moments, Michael repeated, "It's not about you." I started a third time. Michael cut me off sooner, "It's not about you." This repeated two or three more times. I couldn't fully grasp what Michael was saying. I left the tent wondering about what had just happened.

Then I encountered another man I needed to see. He was the director of the Emergency Department at the local hospital. As it turns out, he is also a volunteer with the Bassett Rescue Squad. I approached him to share a perspective that some members of my family had about the accident. You see, the accident occurred around 10:06 pm on Friday night (August 21). The date of Bobby and Pam's deaths was not officially recorded until after midnight on Saturday morning (August 22). Some of my family were concerned that Bobby and Pam might have lingered and suffered as a result. I told this man I did not want him to violate any rules, but it sure would bring comfort to my family if they were assured that Bobby and Pam passed instantly and did not suffer. This man provided me that assurance, which I later shared with my family. He explained that it took a while before their bodies were transported to the hospital following the accident and the date and time recorded by the ER physician reflected the August 22 date.

For the balance of the weekend, I continued to ponder what Michael had so emphatically stated. "It's not about you." I began to reflect on the experience that led to me being in court that Monday afternoon. Again, it wasn't my idea. I did not have an inkling of a thought to pay the fine before I got there. "Maybe, it really isn't about me," I thought.

My brother and my wife, for that matter, had tried repeatedly to draw me into a deeper relationship with God and Jesus Christ. I was just not interested. But now, I was beginning to think differently. When Neil Harvey called me on the following Tuesday (November 3), I wondered how much I should say to him about all of this. I remembered thinking about it but being too nervous to reveal it. That day, Mr. Harvey completed his interviews of the trooper and C.J. I can only imagine how painful that must have been for C.J. Mr. Harvey and his photographer met with me later to finish the interview process and take a photograph of me.

On Friday, November 6th, the article first appeared on *The Roanoke Times* website. I did not see it right away. On Saturday morning, I walked into a favorite local eatery, Ruth's Place, located on Route 220 between Boones Mill and Rocky Mount. When I entered the restaurant, a man at the counter looked up from his newspaper and identified me as the man on the front page of the Saturday morning edition. I felt embarrassed. I located the story online and read it in its entirety. I remember thinking how incredible a job Mr. Harvey did in writing the story, given how much material there was to consider and include. It was an accurate reflection of what I had shared with him. He did a good job of capturing the essence of the story. In my spirit, however, I knew that it wasn't complete.

I knew the story wasn't complete, as I had withheld the fact that I was moved to go to the courtroom that day by the Spirit Who dwelled within me. I didn't fully understand it at the time, but I drove 25 minutes the opposite direction to my workplace that morning. Truthfully, I did not want to go to court that day. It certainly was not my idea to the pay the fine. And I had no idea that I would be included in the proceedings, much less asked to speak.

The article appeared in that Saturday morning's edition on the front page, above the fold. I learned that there is significance to an article appearing above the fold. The other articles included on the front page of the newspaper that day included an article about President Obama, a story about the Russian airliner that was brought down in Egypt, and an article about Ben Casey. The balance of the article appeared on Page 4 of Section A.

Once this article appeared in print and online, it hit the social media platforms, especially Facebook, in a wave. Again, I was not familiar with social media. I had kept myself at arms-length from it. I just did not understand it. My wife would show me the responses that people were having to the story. My youngest brother would text me screenshots of how the story was being shared and the reactions of people. I simply could not wrap my mind around it.

Routinely, I was learning of where other newspapers, most affiliated with the parent company of *The Roanoke Times*, were running abbreviated versions of the story that first appeared on November 6th and 7th.

One day, I was completing an online search and I came across an article on a newspaper's website from Albert Lea, Minnesota. It had first appeared on November 10th, 2015. The article was not a reprint or an excerpt of the main story. Rather, this was an editorial reflecting upon this act of forgiveness. The editorial was titled, *"Would you be able to forgive after crash?"* I was intrigued that this was appearing in a Minnesota newspaper and was reflecting our family's story. I then discovered that the editor had ties to Roanoke.

I reached out to the editor via email and informed her that I had seen the editorial. This prompted a follow-up story about the manner in which news travels. It was interesting to me to say the least.

On September 2nd, 2016, I had another communication with this newspaper editor. She shared with me that two months ago to the day, her eight-year-old child had been riding a bicycle. An elderly man operating a vehicle had accidentally hit the child on the bicycle, resulting in the death of her child. The editor, the child's mother, shared with me that the only thing that was getting her and her family through their situation was their faith, and knowing how God had guided our family through forgiveness, toward healing.

"But without faith it is impossible to please him: for he that cometh to God must believe that he is, and that he is a rewarder of them that diligently seek him."
Hebrews 11:6 (KJV)

CHAPTER 6

LOVE GOD...LOVE PEOPLE!

MATTHEW 22:35-40 (KJV)

"Then one of them, which was a lawyer, asked him a question, tempting him, and saying, Master, which is the great commandment in the law? Jesus said unto him, Thou shalt love the Lord thy God with all thy heart, and with all thy soul, and with all thy mind. This is the first and great commandment. And the second is like unto it, Thou shalt love thy neighbour as thyself. On these two commandments hang all the law and the prophets."

As C.J. and I left the courtroom to go pay the clerk on Monday, October 26th, C.J. put a hand on my shoulder and shook my right hand with his. He asked me how my mom was doing. He asked me how my niece was doing. Then, he invited me to church. "Won't you come to my church?" he asked.

Due to working the NASCAR race event at the Martinsville Speedway on October 31st and November 1st, I could not go that first weekend. I did decide to go on Sunday, November 8th. Did I mention I was apprehensive about going? Remember, I had not been to a church in years. I don't like saying it like this, but the idea of attending a black church made me nervous. The thought of attending the church pastored by the man involved in the accident especially weighed heavy on me. *Did he really mean to invite me? Or, was he just being nice?*

I did not know where C.J.'s church was located for certain, and I didn't know what time the service began. How did they dress there? What should I bring with me? I had lots of questions. I left for church very early on the morning of November 8th. I arrived at the church parking lot before 8:00 am and pulled into the mostly-empty parking lot in the plaza where his storefront church was located. I saw the Sunday School and service times listed on the front door. Sunday School was at 10:00 am and the church service at 11:00 am.

I sat in my car in the parking lot to wait. As I sat there, I began to experience thoughts like, *Who do you think you are? You don't belong here. The people of this church don't want you here.* After a few minutes, my anxiety level was ramping up, so I started my car and left the parking lot. I decided to drive to the scene of the accident and visit the roadside markers that had been placed by T.R.A.S.H. Ministry the night of the funeral. I had never visited the accident scene. As you may recall, it was within sight of the front door of C.J.'s church.

I pulled into the parking lot across from where the markers had been erected. As I got out of the car, tears began to well up in my eyes. I crossed the road to the shoulder where the crosses stood. I stood over them and talked to my brother. I prayed. I cried. I did not know what I was supposed to do. After a brief time, I returned to my car and drove back to the church parking lot.

Here I was again. Sitting and waiting. Waiting for someone to arrive and open the church. I wondered how I would even introduce myself. As I sat there, the thoughts I had previously got stronger. *You haven't been to church in all these years. Why start now? The court case is over. Let these people get on with their lives and you get on with your life. They really do not want you to be here. You will make a fool of yourself. Go on home.*

Once again, I started my car and I left. I was not at all familiar with the areas of Bassett, Fieldale, or Collinsville. I just drove around. My spirit was crying out, asking what I should do. My emotions were telling me to get onto Route 220 and drive north until I reached home. But instead, I found my way back to the church for a third time. When I pulled into the parking lot this time, I noticed a tall black man unlocking the front door of the church. His name is Demetris Childress. He is a deacon at the church. I took a deep breath and mustered all the energy I could and exited my vehicle. I walked into the church. I was warmly greeted by Mr. Childress. He told me that Sunday School would begin momentarily, and I could take a seat in the sanctuary. As it turned out, they used their sanctuary for Sunday School also. Before long, people began filing in for the day's lesson.

Deacon Troy Hairston led Sunday School that morning. You could tell that this man loved teaching, loved his Lord and Savior, and believed in the Bible. As it turns out, in addition to being the pastor of this church, C.J. also worked as an electrician on the night shift for a manufacturing facility in Henry County. He had to work the night before, so he was not able to attend Sunday School, but he arrived at the church about 10:35. When he entered, he immediately recognized me. I kind of stuck out. C.J. made a straight line toward me. I stood up and hugged him for just a minute, then Deacon Troy continued his lesson, and Pastor C.J. exited the sanctuary to go to his study.

At about 11:00 am, Pastor C.J. reentered the sanctuary and took his place at the altar. He attempted to introduce me to his congregation. As he tried to speak my name, his voice cracked, and his lips quivered. I got out of my seat and went to the altar. I grabbed him up in a quick bear hug and told him again, "I've got you, brother. Everything is going to be alright." I quickly turned to go back to my seat only to be greeted by a single file line. Every person in the church building had assembled down the center aisle. They all wanted to give me a hug before they would let me sit back down. It was an absolutely incredible experience, one I could not have anticipated. It showed me the love of this church body.

I did not know the lyrics to the songs they sang for worship. I was a little bit nervous about that. They did not sing from hymnals. They did not have their song lyrics projected onto a wall. I just had to figure it out as we went along.

Then, I heard C.J. preach his message. The first one I had heard in a long time. The first I had ever heard from him. The first to which I could remember the title. The title was, *"Obedience Brings Blessings."* I seemed to hang on every word he preached that day. He was a powerful speaker. I remember him talking about how he had lived much of his life according to what he understood God's will was for his life. He talked about how his blessings were being stored up during this time. He spoke of how those very blessings were poured out over his life in these recent months.

I reflected upon what I heard. I considered the way I lived my life was nearly the opposite. I was not certain I had ever done anything in obedience to God's will for my life. Who could really know such a thing anyway? In any case, in instances where I even imagined I was being obedient, I would call out for God's blessings to be poured out onto me in an instant. I viewed it more like an ATM transaction than being stored up for a future need.

In a moment, I knew that my life was about to take off on a different trajectory. Things were going to be different.

After the service, I made my way to the front where C.J. was standing. I walked up to him and put my arm around his shoulders. I said, "I cannot explain this to you right now, but I have been prepared my whole life for this moment." We exchanged other pleasantries. We told each other we loved one another. And C.J. invited me back for the service the next Sunday.

As I moved to leave the church building, one of the deacons, Jacoby Stanley, called for me to come over. As I approached Deacon Stanley, he put his arm around my shoulder and told me to look at every person who remained in the church. He instructed me to look at their faces. He said, "Our church is less than two years old. If you, your family, and T.R.A.S.H. Ministry had not interceded on behalf of our pastor the way you did, there is no way our church could have continued. All of these people would have been negatively impacted. You have touched the lives of each person here. Don't ever forget this."

Four words are painted above the altar at that church. C.J. often says it is not a motto, but a way of living. He says, "At this church, we will 'Love God...Love People!'" And they sure do live that out. I experienced it first-hand that day. All my apprehension, all my fear, all my doubt, all my insecurity — all of it was washed away in that time with my new House of Purpose family.

I was of a different race. They loved me anyway. I was not a church-attending Christian. They loved me anyway. I didn't know the words to the songs. They loved me anyway. I was not familiar with their worship style. They loved me anyway. I didn't know how to pray. They loved me anyway. I was not familiar with their Sunday School materials. They loved me anyway. It was a powerful experience.

I remember thinking at one point that morning, this is what my brother tried to show me. *This is what he knew and what he wanted to share with me.*

The following Sunday, I returned to House of Purpose. This time, I was not alone. On the second Sunday I attended, November 15th, 2015, my brother's daughter (my niece) and her family attended with me. And, my mom also joined us. They experienced the same outpouring of love on that day that I had seven days prior.

As pastor finished delivering his message that morning, he stepped to the front of the altar and paused. He said, "I've got to get real with everybody in here. In the days and weeks after the accident, the devil was coming at me hard. *I didn't belong in the pulpit. I didn't deserve a ministry. In fact, I didn't deserve to live."* He went on to say, "Every time I was being pushed toward an edge, the Clark Family or T.R.A.S.H. Ministry would show up. It was if God was using the Clark and Quesinberry (my niece's married name) families and T.R.A.S.H. Ministry to reach down, lift me up, and save my life."

When he finished speaking, my 78-year-old mother stood up on one side of the church. C.J.'s 86-year-old mother stood up on the other side of the church and they met in the center aisle. The two of them shared a warm embrace and whispered to one another. Though no one else could hear what they said, it is certain that those words were words of life, love, and healing. The entire congregation stood and gave them an ovation for showing us the way.

Pastor then called out and said, "Brother Clark, is there anything you want to say?"

I approached the altar and took the hand-held microphone from C.J. I stepped up onto the altar. I surrendered my heart, my soul, and my mind once and for all to my Savior, Jesus Christ. I declared him to be my Savior, and Lord over my life. I told those in attendance, "I have been a lukewarm Christian, at best, my entire life. From now on, all that changes. From now on, here am I. Send me." The truth of the matter is you would have had to heat me up just to get to lukewarm. I knew that something was very different after that decision.

When you stand in front of witnesses and you call out to God, "Here I am, Send me," you better put on your seat belt. In my experience, He will hear that and begin to move in your life. I had no idea what I had signed up to. I just knew that I could not live a self-centered, isolated, care-only-about-me kind of existence any more.

From that time, I would call House of Purpose my home church. I would call C.J. Martin my pastor.

When I arrived home from church later that afternoon, I immediately went to my wife to tell her what had happened. Before I could say anything, I noticed that Terri Lee had an expressive look upon her face. It wasn't a look suggesting anger or anxiety. It was one of hesitancy. She appeared as though she had something to say to me but didn't want to speak.

After a few minutes of coaxing, she said, "I just got off the phone with Whitney. I have something I need to tell you, but you cannot get upset." My mind immediately began racing, wondering what she had to say. Terri Lee proceeded to say, "Whitney got a tattoo on her arm. I don't think you will be upset by it though. It was only two words." I asked her what those words were. She replied, "SEND ME." I began to laugh. Terri Lee was surprised, yet relieved at my reaction. My wife did not yet know what I had proclaimed at House of Purpose earlier that day.

After I explained to Terri Lee what had happened at the conclusion of the service, we looked at one other in amazement. Whitney's tattoo was a reminder from God of what He was asking from me, of the calling He had placed on my life.

"Finally, brethren, farewell. Be perfect, be of good comfort, be of one mind, live in peace; and the God of love and peace shall be with you."
2 Corinthians 13:11 (KJV)

CHAPTER 7

A VISIT TO T.R.A.S.H. MINISTRY

1 PETER 5:14 (KJV)

"Greet ye one another with a kiss of charity.
Peace be with you all that are in Christ Jesus. Amen."

On Friday night, November 13th, I made my way to T.R.A.S.H. Ministry for church service for the very first time, ever. This church conducts their weekly services on a Friday night for two reasons: One, to give those who attend a Friday night venue. And, two, to keep the weekends clear so that they can ride their motorcycles.

Walking into this church building, I felt every bit as out of place as I had when I attended House of Purpose for the first time. The biker culture was foreign to me. I didn't ride motorcycles. I never had a desire to do so. From the moment I entered the church, the people were so warm and welcoming. Many of them did not know who I was, and I chose not to say anything, although a few did recognize me.

I grabbed a seat in the sanctuary about four rows from the front on the right side next to the center aisle. I listened to the worship band play. They sang songs that were oddly familiar to me. The music itself was familiar, the lyrics were not. As it turns out, they take popular rock and roll songs and "recycle" them with Christian lyrics. It was very popular with those in attendance. In fact, the name of their worship band is "Recycled."

Pastor Mike Price preached that evening. He is a powerful, charismatic speaker. He preaches much in the same vein as C.J. I struggled to focus on the message. I looked around and wondered where Bobby and Pam had sat before the accident. I looked at all the faces and wondered with whom they had interacted. A couple of times during the service, I saw Mike Price look at me. I wondered if he recognized me. What would I say if he called me to come forward? There was much I wanted to say, but I wasn't sure if the timing was right.

Following the service, pastor Mike came up to me and gave me a hug. He told me he had seen me come into the sanctuary. He said he did not want to call me out during the service. "Bobby hated when I would call him out," he said. I understood. I told him I had something to say to the folks at T.R.A.S.H. And we would know when the timing was right. Then Mike invited me to his office.

We entered a small room off of the Fellowship Hall. He sat in his chair and I sat on a small couch. He talked about how good it was to see me there. He spoke to me about his love for my brother. He said he did not get to talk to Bobby following the service the night of the accident. He said Bobby and Pam had been sitting in the back toward one side. Mike said that at the close of service that night, as was routinely the case, many of the people there wanted to speak with him, so there wasn't an opportunity to speak to Bobby that night. Mike said that Bobby threw his big paw up into the air as if to say, "Great word tonight, brother. I love you. I will see you next time." And then they left.

Mike then asked me, "Do you know anything about lineage ministry?" I laughed.

I responded, "Mike, not only do I not know anything about lineage ministry, I don't know much about anything when it comes to the Bible."

He shared with me some scripture from the Old Testament about the prophet Elijah and a servant named Elisha. Mike explained that Elisha's ministry would not begin in earnest until after Elijah was no longer on this earth. While Elijah was a great prophet and had a powerful ministry, Elisha's would become even more so. Mike concluded by saying, "You will have a ministry that exceeds that of your brother." I knew from this moment that Mike would also be my pastor. I was blessed with two incredible Men of God that would serve to mentor me.

Once again, I could not wrap my mind around all that he was saying to me. As we sat there, we even kicked around ideas for a name. Mike said, "Us on our bikes, we often use the phrase, 'Let's meet at the Crossing.'" From there the idea for My Brothers' Crossing was born. It was 1:30 am by the time I left the church that night.

Sometimes people mistakenly refer to the ministry as *My Brother's Crossing*. Initially, people think that I am speaking specifically of Bobby in my use of the word "brother." Truthfully, the ministry was named using the plural possessive of the word brother. *Brothers'* is written in the plural possessive form and is not actually intended to be a reference to Bobby Clark. In fact, it is not even intended to apply only to men. This grammar is meant to apply to all of us who have been impacted or touched by the tragedy and God's movement through it all – the Martin Family, the Quesinberry Family, the Clark Family, T.R.A.S.H. Ministry and H.O.P. Ministries, the trooper, the first responders, the witnesses, and all who have heard the story and its message of love and hope, obedience and forgiveness.

The next week (November 20th), I attended T.R.A.S.H. Ministry again. I arrived a bit earlier this night and had a chance to speak with Mike before the service started. I told him I had a message I wanted to share with those in attendance. He agreed that he would invite me to come up and speak.

At the conclusion of the sermon, Mike introduced me to everyone and told them I had something to say to them. I approached the front of the church. I took the microphone from him and began to speak. "My name is J.T. Clark. I am Bobby and Pam's brother and brother-in-law. As most of you are aware, they attended this church the night they were killed. They left the church to make their way home to Floyd. But they were called home to be with our Lord and Savior in heaven. I want to acknowledge what you all collectively did for our family that night. You showed up and interceded on behalf of our family. You stood in the gap before we even knew there was an accident. On behalf of my entire family, I want you to know that we love you. You all will always have a special place in our hearts and family."

It felt so good to say that to this group. I wasn't sure how well I would be able to speak. I was certain I would break down in the process of sharing what was on my heart. But God gave me the strength necessary to get through it.

As the service concluded, Mike made an announcement to his congregation that I did not hear clearly. They were planning to meet somewhere on that Sunday (November 22nd) and go somewhere. I did not catch what he said and figured it did not concern me. I didn't think about it any further.

As I attended T.R.A.S.H. Ministry on Friday night and then House of Purpose on Sunday, I discovered something that was remarkable to me. It seemed as if pastor Mike and pastor C.J. delivered eerily similar messages on the same weekend. I even joked that there must be some secret website they use to prepare their messages. They assured me that they gave a common message, because both delivered their sermons based on the guidance and leading of the Holy Spirit.

On Sunday, November 22nd, I was attending Sunday School at House of Purpose. As the morning's class came to a close, the front door of the church opened and a whole group of folks from T.R.A.S.H. Ministry walked in, led by Mike and his wife, Stephanie. The sanctuary was full of a diverse group of people who had come to worship the God we all served. My heart was so full. I began to feel a deep appreciation for my part of this story. My brother's passing served to save my life. But it was also serving as a vehicle for bringing people together. Powerful.

"We are bound to thank God always for you, brethren, as it is meet, because that your faith groweth exceedingly, and the charity of every one of you all toward each other aboundeth."
2 Thessalonians 1:3 (KJV)

CHAPTER 8

WILL YOU COME SPEAK?

Exodus 4:10 (KJV)

"And Moses said unto the LORD, O my LORD, I am not eloquent, neither heretofore, nor since thou hast spoken unto thy servant: but I am slow of speech, and of a slow tongue."

At the time of the accident, I was not what I would call a public speaker. The idea of speaking in public in front of audiences was interesting to me though. There is a verse in the Bible, Proverbs 17:28, that in the King James Version, reads, *"Even a fool, when he holdeth his peace, is counted wise: and he that shutteth his lips is esteemed a man of understanding."* Abraham Lincoln is credited with, "Better to remain silent and be thought a fool than to speak and to remove all doubt." I generally chose not to speak publicly. In fact, as the executive director of the federally-funded healthcare coalition where I was employed, I would delegate such opportunities to others on my team.

That being said, I received a phone call from Michael Harrison. Yes, the Michael Harrison who had impressed upon me, "It's not about you." He was calling to ask if I would be available to attend his church, The Community Fellowship, on November 29th, 2015. He wanted me to share the testimony of what had happened. This service was just more than a month after the court date. It was just less than a month since I'd had my encounter with Michael at the racetrack. I was incredibly excited and nervous all at once.

What if I showed up and said something inappropriate? What if I couldn't hold it together? Who am I that I should be talking to others? I don't even like to speak in public. These thoughts raced through my mind.

When I arrived at The Community Fellowship that morning, people quickly made Terri Lee, our youngest daughter, Whitney, and I feel comfortable. We were invited to sit wherever we wanted. Pastor Harrison explained his plan for the service. He indicated that he would have two bar stools placed at the altar. He said we would just have a question and answer style discussion. He would ask me questions and invite me to speak about what had occurred.

As it turns out, this style of service suited me very well. I was so thankful for the format. It allowed me to catch my breath and compose myself between questions. I was not alone or isolated for this first delivery. The testimony was well received.

Since then, invitations to speak at churches, conferences, customer appreciation events, and other community events have come in waves. The message I have been given an opportunity to share resonates across denominations. I have been invited to speak at Baptist, Methodist, Brethren, Episcopal, and Presbyterian churches. I have spoken to people of the Catholic faith, youth groups, and at nursing facilities. While I have not included every single speaking opportunity that I have experienced since that day at Michael Harrison's church, here are some that I wanted to highlight.

Cedar Springs Union Church: Pastor Neal Turner, a man I had spoken to the day after the accident, invited me to speak at his church on February 14th, 2016. It was a perfect date. As tragic as this story is, it really is a love story. This speaking opportunity was unique because it was the only time I ever asked to speak. When I mentioned to Neal that I would be interested, his response was, "I didn't know you did that (speak at churches)." I replied, "Neither did I know it."

House of Purpose/F.I.R.E. Friday: The third time I was invited to speak for a church service it was at House of Purpose (H.O.P.). A church I would soon call my home church. H.O.P. episodically hosts Friday night services that they call F.I.R.E. Friday. The abbreviation means "Fuel for Inspiring, Restoring, and Exciting God's people to new levels." I was invited there on February 19th to share the testimony that had been birthed in my life.

To say that I was nervous would be an understatement. The people of this church had opened their hearts up to me. What if my words came across as self-righteous or offensive in any way? What if what I shared hurt our pastor in any way?

Once we arrived at the church, C.J. and his wife escorted me back to C.J.'s study. He looked me in the eye and said, "I want you to have full liberty this evening. You say whatever you feel led to say or that you need to say. Do not hold anything back. Do not worry about me or Fernanda. You do what you came here to do." Then they prayed over me. Powerful. We returned to the sanctuary. After a time of worship, I was introduced. I stepped up to the altar. I looked out over the people who had gathered. The room was pretty full. There, sitting on the front row, right in front of me, was Pastor C.J. Martin and his wife, Fernanda. They made eye contact with me through the entire service. The look that they shared back with me was one of love and compassion. I shared the story that had already unfolded in our lives. I will never forget the experience of that evening. Simply amazing!

Charlottesville Church of the Brethren: Returning home from a church service where I spoke on March 6th, I received a message from dear family friends, Tom and Dottie Williams, whom I had not spoken with in over a decade. They wanted to know if I could speak at their church in Charlottesville. They were organizing a special service on April 17th, 2016. They intended this service to also feature a message about depression and mental health concerns. The God moment in this exchange was that for the first time, publicly, I had spoken that morning (March 6th) to a Sunday School class about my thirty-year battle with depression and suicidal ideation. The very day that I revealed that for the first time, I was given an opportunity to follow it up.

Slate Mountain Presbyterian Church: Pastor Jeff Dalton invited me to speak at his church on April 10th, 2016. Pastor Jeff had known my brother well. He spoke at the funeral service. He worked in public safety, serving as a Captain of the Floyd County Sheriff's Department. The day before I was to speak at his church, I was at work. It was a Saturday afternoon around 4:40 pm. I had just started to listen to a Christian Radio Station, known as The Journey, based in Lynchburg, VA. As I was working, I heard a clip of a song that was not familiar. It was a contemporary Christian song by Matthew West entitled, "Forgiveness." As this clip of the song played, a man's spoken testimony was embedded in the song. As I heard it, I thought,

Oh my! That guy has been through the same thing I have been through. A split-second later, I realized it was my voice. It was my story. I was hearing myself within the song, "Forgiveness," airing on the radio. That evening, I contacted the general manager of the radio station, Barry Armstrong. I told him I was speaking at a church the next morning and needed a copy of the audio clip. I received it later that evening and played it at the end of the service at Pastor Jeff's church. I have used it in every service since that day.

Little Fork Episcopal Church: This service was very special. This is an historic church that my sister, Susan Brown, calls her home church. The service was on May 1st, 2016. This service represented the first time so many of my family heard me speak. My niece, Aby, served as an acolyte for the service. Following the service, light refreshments were served in the fellowship hall and I was invited to engage in a question and answer session. A woman raised her hand and asked, "So how soon before you are writing a book about all of this?" It was the first time I had been asked publicly about writing a book.

Craig County Churches: On April 13th, 2016, I stopped at a Bojangles restaurant on my way to work that morning. Normally, I would just go to the drive-thru. On this day, I went inside and sat in the restaurant to eat. Bojangles is a fast-food restaurant that features, chicken, biscuits, and sweet tea. As I ate my breakfast, I noticed a woman sitting in the booth just in front of me. There were three men sitting at a table across the restaurant to my left. As I finished my meal and went to empty the tray, I heard, "Tell those men your story." I looked at my watch and thought, I don't have time for this. I need to get to work. As I headed toward the exit, I heard, "It's not too late. Turn around." As I exited the building and walked across the parking lot, I heard, "It's not too late. Turn around." As I got into my vehicle and started the engine, I heard it again. As I exited the parking lot to turn onto the roadway, I heard it again. As I drove away from the restaurant, I heard it a final time, "It's not too late. Turn around." By the time I was a mile away, I stopped hearing it. Instantly, I was disappointed. I knew that I failed to be obedient to what I was being called to do. With all that has happened, how could I choose to be disobedient to this request?

The next morning, I was two exits short of my destination. I took that exit and drove to a Chick-fil-A restaurant. I never frequent this particular establishment as I have a Chick-fil-A restaurant more directly on my route of travel from home. I parked my vehicle and went inside. It was breakfast time and I waited for my turn to order. A man asked if he could take my order. I approached the counter and told him what I wanted. As he placed the food on my tray, I picked it up and turned around to find a table. As I turned around, I heard, "Tell this man your story." Now I was at a Chick-fil-A restaurant at breakfast time. This guy didn't have time for me to tell him my story. I could not just stand there at the counter and talk with him. I took one step away from the counter, and I heard, "Don't you remember what happened yesterday at the Bojangles?" I turned 180 degrees and placed my tray back on the counter. I said, "Sir, God is telling me to tell you a story." He replied, "I'm all ears." I stood at the counter for 15 – 20 minutes sharing as much of the story as I could. As I talked to him, tears welled up in his eyes and streamed down his cheeks. Not a single customer approached the counter the entire time. When I finished I said, "I don't know in what I just said that you needed to hear, but God wanted me to tell you this story." This man, Gary Burch, a manager at this Chick-fil-A, wiped the tears away and replied, "I know exactly what I needed to hear. I am a pastor at two churches in Craig County and I will need you to speak at each church one Sunday in the near future." On Sunday, May 8th, I spoke at both churches.

Colonial Avenue Baptist Church: I spoke at this church on June 19th, 2016. The service began at 10:00 am. I needed to be in Floyd County by 3:00 pm. The day's program at this church was very full as they were celebrating graduates, the end of Vacation Bible School, and then I was invited to speak. A couple who had first heard me speak on February 14th at Neal Turner's church had traveled to Roanoke to hear me speak for the fourth time. The wife shared that my story was having an impact on them. She said, "I cannot tell you about it yet, but the day will come. One day, I will be able to reveal it to you." The reason I needed to be in Floyd by 3:00 pm was for a baptismal service. You see, the man who was driving the pick-up truck involved in the accident with Bobby and Pam…he was coming to Floyd that afternoon to baptize their two youngest grandchildren. Not only was June 19th Father's Day, not only was he coming to baptize them in the same waterway where my brother had baptized his other grandchildren, but it also would have been Bobby and Pam's 40th wedding anniversary. You can't make this stuff up.

Fundraiser for the family of Bubba Creasy: On July 24th, 2016, I was invited to speak at *The Little White Church* in Floyd County. Following the service, one of the leaders, Michael Zeman, told me that he was really sorry one of their founding members, Bubba Creasy, could not be there to hear it. He told me that Bubba was ill with cancer. He indicated that they were planning a fundraiser to help offset some of the expenses relating to his treatment. He asked me if I would be available to speak at this fundraiser for Mr. Creasy and his family on Saturday, August 13th. As Michael stood there speaking with me, his wife, Leigh Ann, approached. She told Michael that they needed to leave for the hospital. She had received word that Bubba had been readmitted. Two days later, July 26th, I received word that Bubba had died. I did not know him. I had never met him or his family. But I reached out to Michael and said, "I understand that Bubba has passed. I am certain you will continue with the fundraiser as the need is just as big. My wife and I will be coming to support the event. Considering his death, if you decide that you would rather me not speak, I understand." Without hesitation he told me he absolutely wanted me to speak.

From that day until Thursday, August 11th, I wondered, *What is the connection? I do not know this man nor his family. How am I connected to all of this?* Around 4:00 pm on August 11th, I was leaving Lynchburg General

70

Hospital. The organization in which I was employed had participated in a tabletop disaster exercise at the hospital. As I climbed into my vehicle to make the 90-minute drive home, my telephone rang. It was my niece, Robin, my brother's daughter. She asked me if I was going to be speaking in Floyd this weekend. I responded that I was. She shared that she would be out of town, but that she really wished she could be there. Robin had attended a handful of these engagements in support of me. There was something in her voice that told me there was something different about this engagement. I asked her about the significance. She said, "I was Bubba Creasy's home care nurse before he was admitted to the hospital. I had been caring for him right before his death." I now knew the connection between our story and this man and his family. I would meet another man that night who I would stay connected with through all of this. His name was Andy Bandy. He was invited to sing during the evening's program with a trio of other singers.

Wylliesburg Baptist Church: On Tuesday, October 4th, the organization where I work, the Near Southwest Preparedness Alliance (NSPA), had deployed an asset in support of the Vice-Presidential debate hosted at Longwood University in the town of Farmville. I had an understanding that we would have until the following weekend to retrieve the 28' trailer from the university and return it to Roanoke. On the morning of October 5th, I learned that the trailer needed to be removed from the campus that day. I was not available to make the trip and I did not have a staff member available to handle this assignment. My next option was to find a local company in Farmville to tow the trailer back to the Roanoke area for me. After three attempts, I finally spoke with a woman named Amy at Spurlock's Garage. She was certain they could handle the work. It took a total of six telephone conversations to work out all the details. Each time I spoke with Amy, I felt a message come over my spirit, "Tell her your story." I resisted. *I don't know this woman. She is at work trying to do her job and I am at work trying to do mine.* I chose not to say anything.

In the early evening, I met the tow truck driver at our storage lot. As we greeted one another, I asked him, "Do you know Amy who works at the garage?" He replied, "I reckon I ought to. She's my wife." I laughed and told him that I think I was supposed to tell her a story. I told him I didn't want to interfere with her work, but that I had half-a-mind to call her Thursday morning to tell her. He encouraged me to go ahead. At 9:03 am on Thursday, I was standing in my driveway and I telephoned Amy. I said, "Ma'am, it has been on my spirit that I needed to tell you a story. I know you're probably busy and I don't mean to keep you. When I tell you this story, you may think I am crazy. If that's the case, you hang up. If you need to tend to some other task, we can arrange a time to talk later. If you have a few minutes now, I will give you a short version." She encouraged me to tell her. I told her about a ten-minute version. When I got to the end, I said, "I don't know what you needed to hear in all that, but there was something in it for you." She replied, "I know exactly what I needed to hear. At the top of my 'to-do' list for today was to finalize speakers for a special revival service at my church, Wylliesburg Baptist Church. I need you to speak on Tuesday, October 25th." That would be the first of three times that I would speak there.

Stonewall House of Prayer: On August 13th, while listening to the musical talent that was performing at the fundraiser event for the family of Bubba Creasy, I stood to exit the church. My wife and I wanted to step outside where she could pray over me before I stepped into the pulpit. As I exited the row to the outer aisle, I turned and saw a man who had been sitting directly behind me. It was Dan Whitlock. Dan is the pastor at *Stonewall House of Prayer.* Dan and his wife, Sabrina, had been riding their motorcycle with my brother the night of the accident. Dan and Bobby were brothers in their faith walk, in their ministry work, and in the way they lived their lives. Dan immediately recognized me and jumped to his feet to give Terri Lee and me a hug. After the service that night, Dan said to me, "I had no idea you were out speaking and sharing this testimony." He said, "I need to have you at my church." On November 6th, 2016, Terri Lee and I attended *Stonewall House of Prayer* to speak for the first of three times.

Richmond Area Youth Retreat at the Eagle Eyrie Center: On August 7th, 2016 I had the privilege of speaking at Ramsey Memorial United Methodist Church in Richmond, VA. Erin Shrader-Amason had collaborated with then pastor, Deborah Koontz, on a special Sunday evening dinner and service. A man in attendance had served as the adult leader for the Richmond Area Youth Retreat for 20 years. In the upcoming year, he was going to serve as a special advisor to Robert Smith who was taking the reins for the 2017 offering. When the youth leadership met in October to discuss their theme for the February 2017 event, an option that surfaced was Forgiveness. The special advisor informed the collective that if forgiveness was a theme they wanted to pursue, he might know a featured speaker for the event.

Chapter 8: *Will You Come Speak?*

They did choose forgiveness for their theme and I was invited to speak, along with C.J. Martin and Mike Price. As it turns out, Mike's schedule would not allow for him to participate. Initially, C.J. was not available either. At the last minute, his situation changed, and he committed to joining me. On Saturday morning, February 18th, C.J. and I were introduced and invited to speak to those in attendance, numbering 350 or so. My mother, Nancy, was in attendance, along with Fernanda, (C.J.'s wife), and Terri Lee. We started with some light-hearted banter and then I began to share the story as I had hundreds of times before. To my knowledge, this was C.J.'s first time to speak publicly about it to an audience who was not already familiar with the story. It proved to be difficult and therapeutic at the same time. At the conclusion of the morning service, C.J. and his wife retreated to the room that had been provided for them at the conference center. I was uncertain as to whether he was going to be up to joining me for the evening service. Shortly after noon, I received a call from C.J. He asked me to stop by their room. It was a short distance from where I was to their room, but it was a long walk. When I arrived, I hesitantly knocked on their door. Fernanda swung the door open wide and there the two of them stood with smiles on their faces as wide as Texas. Instantly, I knew that he was recovering. C.J. asked me what the plan was for the evening service. I explained that I thought we would continue the story and see how we were led by the Holy Spirit. He said, "I have an idea to do a demonstration." I thought that was great and was excited to receive confirmation that he was in fact going to rejoin me on the stage that evening.

C.J. and Fernanda went into Lynchburg to get a few supplies for the demonstration he was planning. Before entering the venue, our wives joined C.J. and me just outside. They wanted to pray over us before we addressed the audience. Following a brief time of prayer, the four of us shared a moment of love and joy. It was uplifting and celebratory. The adult leader, Rob Smith, witnessed what was taking place. He said, "I wish we could open this (exterior) wall up right here so that everyone inside could witness the authenticity of the relationship out here. As we took the stage Saturday evening, we again exchanged in some back-and-forth commentary. C.J. directed me to finish sharing the testimony, picking up from where we left off in the morning. As we neared the end, C.J. took center stage. He addressed the crowd in a spirited manner. He then reached in his bag for the items he needed for his demonstration. He placed a 9" X 9" plastic tray on the stage floor. He then retrieved a half-dozen raw eggs.

He talked about the fragility of life and compared it to the raw eggs. As he bounced an egg in his hand, he spoke, "If T.R.A.S.H. Ministry hadn't showed up on the scene that night…he spiked an egg into the plastic tray…THUD…that would have been me." He grabbed a second egg, "If Robin and Greg hadn't called me on Sunday…THUD…that would have been me." If J.T. hadn't been obedient and showed up in the courtroom… THUD; if House of Purpose hadn't stood with me…THUD; if Momma Clark hadn't showed me a Mother's Love…THUD; if my wife, daughter, son, and family hadn't been there for me…THUD." Then, C.J. reached back into the plastic bag and pulled out a tennis ball. He began bouncing the tennis ball on the stage. He talked about how each time we get knocked down, we have an opportunity to bounce back. At the end, he said, "It's when we get knocked down the hardest that we have the opportunity to bounce back the highest." As he finished those words, he spiked that tennis ball with all his might and the ball bounced 25 feet into the air. There was not a dry eye to be seen and those in attendance erupted in applause and cheers. C.J. would later joke with me, "That was a 'drop-the-mic' moment."

The Fertilizer Warehouse: On March 30th, 2017 I attended this church for the first time. The man who owns *The Fertilizer Warehouse* goes by the nickname Scotty. 18 years prior, Scotty converted this fertilizer warehouse to a church. He held his first, week-long camp meeting there 18 years ago. When you enter the warehouse, you discover that the usual accoutrements of a fertilizer warehouse operation were gone. In their place were wooden pews, an altar, a sound system, and a pulpit. They offer church services at this place each Thursday night. Scotty arranges for musical talent to open the worship portion of the service and then has a guest speaker. The service is bookended by a time of men's fellowship before the service and a potluck dinner afterwards. The first night I showed up at the church, I was with a pastor, Todd Barnes, who was the designated speaker for the evening.

I had only met Todd five days prior when I spoke at his church. Sometime during the evening, Scotty approached Todd and asked him if Todd could vouch for me. Todd told me his response was, "I sure hope so. He just spoke at my church." During the meal, Scotty came up to me and said, "I don't know when I will have an opening, but I would like for you to speak here sometime." To my knowledge, Scotty did not know of the testimony that I had been routinely sharing. Todd told me, "It was something about your spirit that Scotty was drawn to." On May 4th, 2017

Scotty approached me and said, "I need a replacement for the service in three weeks on May 25th. Can you do it?" My calendar was clear, and I eagerly told him that I could. The following week, a local newspaper ran an article that served as an update to the story of the accident, our ministry, and some of what was transpiring as a result. When I entered *The Fertilizer House* that Thursday (May 11th), the newspaper article was taped to the inside of the main entry door. On May 18th (one week before I was to speak) as I stood in line to fix my dinner plate, Eric Ferguson (the speaker on that night) spoke to me. He said, "Scotty wants you to know this. If the Holy Spirit gives you a different message for the service next week, feel free to go as the Holy Spirit leads. You do not have to share your testimony that night."

My reaction was one of surprise. I had never been invited to speak except to share my testimony. I did not know what that would mean. On the 45-minute drive home, I prayed out loud. "God, I don't know what you would have me do. But, if there is something about which you would rather I speak, let me know." On Friday morning, I woke up with a single word in my spirit – obedience. I thought, *Oh, this is good. There are plenty of stories and scripture on this subject. I can certainly pull together a sermon with relative ease.* On Sunday, May 21, Robert Foresman had arranged for me to speak at a church in Lexington, VA, some 90 minutes away from home. When my wife and I returned home that afternoon, I took a nap. When I awoke, I had a message on my spirit. "Can you demonstrate your obedience to Me by standing in the pulpit for 45 minutes and not saying a word?"

"Wait. What?! Did I hear what I thought I just heard? That's funny. The first time I get invited to share a message, you want me to stand in the pulpit and not say a word. I am sure You will give me clarity about this before Thursday." Monday arrived. I did not receive any additional information. I thought, *Okay. Well, at least I need to inform Scotty about what happened. I don't want him to get nervous and pull me out of the pulpit.* The instant I had this thought, I heard, "In order to demonstrate your obedience to me, you cannot share what I have asked you to do with anyone who is going to be there Thursday night." This meant that I could not tell Scotty. I could not discuss it with my wife. I could not talk to C.J. about it as he was arranging his work schedule, so he could attend. On Tuesday, I was really getting worked up about this whole arrangement. I was to "speak" in 48 hours and I did not know what I was going to do. Stand there and not say anything?!

This makes no sense. I know. I will just share my testimony. I have done that so many times, I know I can deliver it. As soon as I had that thought, I heard, "If you share your testimony, it will fall on deaf ears."

Wednesday morning, I woke up full of anxiety. Later in the day, I heard from C.J. He had sent me a message advising that it had not worked out with his employment situation. He would not be able to attend on Thursday evening. I was disappointed, but also excited. Since he couldn't attend, I could tell him what I had been instructed to do. When I told him, he gave me a two-word response, "Trust Him." When I went to bed on Wednesday night, I had a small measure of peace. I did not have anything prepared for Thursday evening. I had resigned myself to the fact that it wasn't in the plan. On Thursday morning, I awoke and was in the shower. As I washed my hair, Psalm 46:10 dropped into my spirit. I did not know what that verse was. I couldn't get out of the shower fast enough. I was dripping over my Bible as I flipped to that chapter. I read it to say, in part, "Be still and know that I am God…" I thought, "Okay, this is how we are going to do this."

That evening, I attended the men's fellowship time. The men in the room were speaking about various thoughts they had about aspects of the Bible. Then, it was time to pray over me. We entered the sanctuary and listened to the musical talent that performed that night. Afterwards, Richard, who routinely serves as Master of Ceremonies, took the microphone to introduce me. Richard was not aware that Scotty had given me liberty to go as the Spirit leads me. Richard had become aware of the testimony that I routinely shared and he teed me up. He began his introduction by telling those in attendance that the next speaker had been traveling all over. "He has been sharing an incredible story of forgiveness. People who have heard it comment that it really impacted them." I was sitting there in disbelief. *Oh no.* Richard did not know. Following the introduction, I approached the pulpit, and took the microphone from Richard. I laid my Bible down and opened it to Psalm 46:10 and I set the microphone down. I stood there in silence. I did not acknowledge the musicians who had performed. I did not thank Richard for the introduction. I did not thank Scotty for inviting me to speak. I stood at the pulpit and began to scan the room. I made eye contact with those in attendance. I scanned the room from left to right and back again. I did this a total of four times. As this continued, things began to break down. I could hear people making comments such as, "Who is he waiting on? Did he forget what he was going to say? Who is he looking at? Is he scared?" Then I heard a woman state, "This is the best sermon I ever heard." It was at this moment that I was moved to read Psalm 46:10, *"Be still, and know that I am God: I will be exalted among the heathen, I will be exalted in the earth."* After reading this, the message began. "Isn't it interesting how we come into God's house on a Thursday night? We invite the Holy Spirit to be with us. We ask that our hearts and spirits be ready to receive a message that God would have for us. I am here to tell you that God had a message for every one of us tonight, believer and non-believer alike. Isn't it interesting that as soon as things get a little out of the norm; if things are different than what we are used to or expect, we get uncomfortable. I am not here to embarrass anyone. I am not going to ask you to raise your hand, but I wonder how many of you heard what God had for you." Following this introduction, it just flowed from there. I am certain it was not the greatest message ever preached in that place, but it didn't matter. I was learning to be obedient to God regardless of what people thought of what I was doing.

Mt. Zion United Methodist Church (Georgetown): Two days after I spoke at *The Fertilizer Warehouse,* I received a telephone call from Reverend Dr. Johnsie Cogman of *Mt. Zion United Methodist Church (Georgetown),* the oldest African-American church in Washington, D.C. I had been anticipating a call from her for several weeks. I was introduced to her through email by way of a man I met in Philadelphia in April at the 2017 NFL Draft. The email introduction seemed to indicate that Reverend Dr. Cogman was interested in having me come to speak, but a telephone call never followed. When we spoke on May 27th, she informed me that she had made an effort to telephone several times in the preceding weeks, but every time she started to call me, something came up. I rationalized that God was wanting to see if I was going to be obedient about the message at *The Fertilizer Warehouse.* Once I demonstrated my obedience there, the next opportunity presented itself.

Rev. Dr. Cogman and I agreed that I would speak on Father's Day during the regular Sunday service. My wife and I traveled up to D.C. the Friday night before and we showed up at an outreach opportunity this church is routinely engaged in to minister to those who are shelter-challenged. It was an honor to serve alongside some incredible people as we ministered to those in need through food and God's Word. It was humbling to stand in this particular church and speak to those in attendance on Sunday morning. The history of this church body included being a part of the Underground Railroad during the 1800's. One of the sweetest surprises that day occurred as I sat at the altar as the service was beginning. I looked in the direction where my wife was seated, and I discovered that C.J. and Fernanda's daughter, Corretta Martin, had made the trip in from Maryland to support me that day. It was very special indeed. When it was announced that I would deliver my Initial Sermon as part of the ordination process at C.J.'s church, Reverend Dr. Cogman's husband, Billy, and his brother arranged to make a 10-hour round trip drive that day, to serve as witnesses to that special day. They said they were so moved by the testimony I shared back in June that they had to send representatives to bear witness to my ordination.

Mount Carmel Baptist Church (Carmel, NY): On June 2 and 3rd, my wife and I were invited to speak at this church in Carmel, N.Y. I had gotten to know the pastor of this church, Andrew Columbia, during the previous 20 months. While Andrew was serving as an evangelist, he and I were scheduled to speak at the same event honoring the military and first responders. From that point, Andrew has served as a special mentor to me. We had been connected through a series of services during this time. In late 2017, Andrew accepted an assignment at this church. He asked Terri Lee and I to come up and minister there. Terri Lee spoke to the Women's Fellowship group on Saturday, while I spoke to the Men's Fellowship group. Then, on Sunday, I spoke during the regular Sunday morning church service.

As I would travel around and share this testimony, a few people would say something to the effect of, "You must not have loved your brother very much to do what you did." The truth of the matter is, "It is because I loved my brother, I was able to do what I did." This is the way Bobby and Pam lived their lives. They would not have wanted us to handle this any differently.

As I have said, I do not believe in coincidences. My unbelief in coincidences has magnified in the time since the accident. There are just far too many variables for this to have been a series of coincidences. The World Wide Web can't begin to compare to the network of God when he chooses to disseminate His message of love and forgiveness. For instance, since my conversation with Neal Turner about speaking at Union Springs

Christian Church on February 14th, 2016, I have never reached out to a single church, ministry, or organization asking if I could come speak. Each speaking opportunity has originated outside of any effort on my part. Each opportunity was created by God as He began His work to bring triumph from tragedy. I have simply vowed to go wherever God makes a way.

"For he whom God hath sent speaketh the words of God: for God
giveth not the Spirit by measure unto him."
John 3:34 (KJV)

CHAPTER 9

I'VE GOT SOMETHING I'VE GOT TO TELL YOU

1 Thessalonians 1:3 (KJV)

"Remembering without ceasing your work of faith, and labour of love, and patience of hope in our Lord Jesus Christ, in the sight of God and our Father."

After sharing this testimony at a church for the third time, I was walking out of the sanctuary and a man who appeared to be with the church leadership thanked me for sharing such an incredible story and message. He shook my hand and handed me an envelope. I accepted the envelope almost quizzically, thanked him for the opportunity to be with them, and headed to my car. Another man, Bob Suddarth, had arranged for me to speak at this church. At the time, this was his home church. Bob is a dear friend of mine. He and Deborah (his wife) and two friends, Joel and Terri, had traveled to hear me speak a couple of weeks before. Bob had arranged for us to have lunch before Terri Lee and I would head home.

As I climbed into my vehicle at the church parking lot, I handed the envelope to my wife. She opened it to reveal a check for $100.00. I was stunned. I didn't know what to say or how to feel about it. In the moment, it was surreal. To be honest, it felt like I was accepting blood money. When we arrived at the restaurant for lunch, a short drive from the church, I walked in with the envelope in my hand. I remember handing it to Bob expressing how humbled I was by the gesture. I explained that I could not accept it. I asked him to return it to his church with my profound appreciation. He agreed.

The next day, I received a telephone call from Bob. He explained that he had done as I requested. He returned the check to the church leadership with my thanks and appreciation. He explained that they would not accept it back. He told me, "They want you to use this for your ministry. I am going to put this in the mail to you." I was stunned. I didn't know how to respond. I had been talking with Mike Price about the formation of a ministry; but, to that point, it was just that – talk. *I don't know anything about this. Who am I to operate a ministry?!*

Six days later, I spoke at another church. Once again, I received an envelope. Over the course of the next several weeks, I would be invited to speak at other churches and venues. People would ask me, "What is your fee to speak?" I had no fee. Frankly, this was confusing for me at the time. Halfway through April, I had amassed over half a dozen checks. I did not know what to do with them. I couldn't bring myself to deposit them or cash them. I was carrying them in my wallet. One morning, my wife came to me and said, "You left your wallet in your pants pocket. That pair of pants went through the wash last night." In addition to the wallet and all its contents, the checks too were wet and damaged. Now what to do?

I asked a colleague, Mike Pruitt, "Who would you speak with about establishing a ministry?" He gave me the name of an attorney in a small town in Franklin County called Rocky Mount (VA). I called his office to schedule an appointment with him. His assistant informed me that his next availability would be Tuesday, June 21st (2016). The day arrived, and I made the trip to his office. I waited in a waiting area of his office half-wondering, "What am I doing here?" The attorney, Eric Ferguson, greeted me and escorted me back to a small conference room. He confessed that he did not fully understand why I had made the appointment. I told him that I was there to discuss with him the process for establishing a ministry. I said, "To fully understand what I am trying to do, I need to tell you a story." I proceeded to tell him all about the night of the accident and what had happened in the courtroom down in Henry County. He listened ever so intently for about 20 minutes as I shared this information with him.

When I finished, Mr. Ferguson, who had been sitting back in his chair as I spoke, leaned up across the table from me and said, "I've got something I have to tell you." From his tone, facial expressions, and body language, I could see this was going to be something incredible. But I had no idea. He said, "I was in the courtroom that day. I was standing there talking with the state trooper when you walked up and interrupted our conversation. My case had already been dealt with during the morning session. I was just talking to the trooper about fishing. When you walked up and interrupted our conversation, I knew I had no further business there. I left. I never knew how that turned out." He went on to share with me a personal matter relating to forgiveness and how the story I had shared with him was causing him to reflect on his own situation. He then informed me that he was going to provide the legal services to start the ministry for free.

Eric, as I have come to know him, and I have continued our relationship. He arranged with his pastor, Todd Barnes, for me to speak at his church on March 26th, 2017. He was the one who had told me about *The Fertilizer Warehouse.* He suggested that we might visit there together sometime. We know from the previous chapter how that worked out.

"But let us, who are of the day, be sober, putting on the breastplate of faith and love; and for an helmet, the hope of salvation."
1 Thessalonians 5:8 (KJV)

CHAPTER 10

COMMEMORATING, SERVING, & CELEBRATING

MATTHEW 22:9 (KJV)

"Go ye therefore into the highways, and as many as ye shall find, bid to the marriage."

As the one-year anniversary of the accident approached, we wanted to join our families and ministries together to remember and celebrate Bobby and Pam. We were certain part of the weekend would include services at both T.R.A.S.H. Ministry and House of Purpose. I was kicking around ideas for what to do on the Saturday in between.

A few weeks before the anniversary, I was attending a service at T.R.A.S.H. on a Friday night. One of the bikers, Ricky, who attends regularly, was invited to share a story about a situation in his home neighborhood, a short distance from the church. He and Pastor Mike talked about a recent visit to the neighborhood. Ricky talked about how the home that belonged to his family had been empty for some time. He spoke of how the home had been broken into and used as a haven for drug activity. Pastor Mike spoke of a little girl they saw walking through the neighborhood carrying a cat. As they shared this story, Ricky said he asked Pastor Mike, "You see that little girl? That cat she is holding may be her only friend." They spoke of the desperate conditions in this neighborhood and wanted to do something to touch the lives of the people who lived there. This neighborhood was reportedly known for gang activity, prostitution, and illegal drugs.

Within a week, a plan was hatched. We were going to use the occasion of the anniversary of the accident to go into this neighborhood to minister to those who lived there. The event would be called, *My Brothers' Crossing Cookout*. The plan included going to Ricky's home property and cleaning it up. Then, we would meet at T.R.A.S.H. on August 20th and move into the neighborhood unannounced. We would show up with coolers of food and gas grills and prepare a picnic for anyone who would come and join us. A couple of folks from the Recycled Band would also play some music. Nearly 100 volunteers participated. Several other churches contributed in different ways when they learned of the plan.

As the set-up got underway, we canvassed the neighborhood. We knocked on the doors of each home in the neighborhood. We invited those who opened their doors to join us at the cookout. Much of the response was tepid interest, at best. As the food was being prepared, two little African-American boys named Xavier and Sincere came over to the food area. I sat down in the grass with them and we each enjoyed a hot dog. As we ate, I spoke to them about their friends in the neighborhood. After they finished, the two boys disappeared back into the neighborhood. They re-emerged with an army of a dozen children. They were sprinting to come and get some food. Before long, the grandparents were coming out of their homes to experience the excitement. By the end of the day, some of the gang members, prostitutes, and drug users had come to take part. We may never know the impact of The Cookout on that neighborhood that day. But what I do know, is that many people received something to eat; some folks chose to take one of the Bibles that we had available; everyone enjoyed a time of fellowship; and folks were shown an example of Christ's love for each person.

The evening before *My Brothers' Crossing Cookout*, we gathered at T.R.A.S.H. Ministry for an evening of praise, worship, fellowship, and to hear God's Word being preached. As is customary at T.R.A.S.H. Ministry, the collection of people was diverse. Toward the end of the service, Pastor Mike began calling individuals to come forward and asked them to take the hand of the person next to him or her. He called on this body of people to continue to be evidence of God's love in the lives of others. It was a powerful way to start the weekend and to end the service.

Sunday marked the one-year anniversary of the accident. The Thursday prior, Pastor C.J. Martin and his wife telephoned me to discuss the message for the service. He told me the title and the theme for the message he believed he was to preach on that Sunday. The title was, *"What do you believe?"* The message would be focused on what we say we believe as Christians, what Bobby and Pam believed as they served Jesus Christ, their Lord and Savior, and how our actions line up with our stated belief. C.J. asked how I thought my family would react to such a message. My response to him was matter-of-fact, "If you believe the Holy Spirit gave you this message, you have no choice. Step out and deliver it."

A very special part of the service that day was a message that First Lady Fernanda Martin had prepared. Toward the end of the service, she stood at the altar and read the following. It was real. It was genuine. It was authentic. With permission from Fernanda Martin, I have included it here.

In 2013, when our ministry was established, we wanted this ministry to be founded on love, "Love God...Love People." Our plan was to show God's love to all people regardless of their status, race, or situation. John 15:12, "This is my commandment, That ye love one another, as I have loved you." And John 13:35: "By this shall all men know that ye are my disciples, if ye have love one to another." We had no idea that our foundation would come to life in such a profound way. We would have never thought the table would be turned on us. The love we have experienced in the past year has made those scriptures rise off the pages of the bible and literally walk right into our hearts.

To our TRASH family: Yes, I must admit my initial encounter with you, I felt our lives were endangered. Little did I know the very people I thought were there to hurt us were the first ones there to love us. We will be forever grateful.

To our Clark family: Words will never be able to express the love we feel for you. The very first time Greg and Robin reached out to us, we didn't quite know what to think. I asked, "How could anyone show someone they didn't know so much love while enduring so much pain and loss?" Love God...Love People. "How could anyone defend someone they never laid eyes on?" Love God...Love People.

The first time Robin and the Clark family came to worship with us I was sitting over in the corner (of the sanctuary) amazed at how awesome God is and what He was doing for our families. God spoke to me that Sunday and said, "Robin has started a revolution." I responded and asked, "A revolution?" God spoke back and said, "Yes, a revolution of love and forgiveness." So, I was very anxious to get home to find the definition of "revolution." Revolution: a dramatic and wide-reaching change in the way something works or people's ideas about it. The love and forgiveness that was extended to us has not only changed our lives, but it has been a wide-reaching change. J.T. had shared with us that it was Robin that set the tone of love and forgiveness and the Clark family followed her lead. The Revolution of Love and Forgiveness flowed into that courtroom that day touching not only our family but all that were present, "wide-reaching change." Whenever J.T. is sharing the message of Love and Forgiveness across the country, where lives are being transformed is just another reminder of The Revolution of Love and Forgiveness that was started by Robin.

Because she dared to step into this revolution, my family is stronger. The House of Purpose foundation is stronger. Our family has increased. Our ministry has increased. Our love and faith have increased. And we absolutely realize that all of this was an extension of Bobby and Pam Clark's love for God. We may not have met Bobby and Pam, but through their lives, love and forgiveness was shown to us and this revolution is spreading like a wildfire. We are honored to say, "It's been a pleasure meeting you, Bobby and Pam."

We love you Robin and the Clark family.

At the conclusion of Sunday's service, I had arranged to have two doves released. This would occur outside the entrance to the church once we were all outside. Robin selected three songs that we would sing as part of the service. All three ministries were represented.

As we stepped outside to release the doves, my mother and Robin were each given a box containing one bird. After a prayer by C.J. and a quick countdown, the boxes were opened to release the birds. The doves left the boxes in opposite directions, one circling counterclockwise and the other clockwise. As they flew overhead, they circled back together over the area of the accident scene and flew off together. It was a moment that was both touching and fitting for the occasion.

Those in attendance commented that this day was one of healing. It served to further bind our families and our ministries together. Fernanda and I shared a moment. I said to her, "We had to find a way to love our way through this."

"But if thou wilt go, do it, be strong for the battle:
God shall make thee fall before the enemy: for God hath power to
help, and to cast down."
2 Chronicles 25:8 (KJV)

CHAPTER 11

PITTSBURGH STEELERS VS. WASHINGTON REDSKINS

Proverbs 27:10 (KJV)

"Thine own friend, and thy father's friend, forsake not; neither go into thy brother's house in the day of thy calamity: for better is a neighbour that is near than a brother far off."

On December 31st, 2015, just over four months after the accident, Greg and Robin (and their daughter Rosln) and Terri Lee and I attended a church party celebrating the Christmas and New Year's holidays. During this party, we were introduced to C.J. and Fernanda's daughter, Corretta. She lives in Maryland and was home visiting for the holidays. That night, I learned that C.J. and his daughter, Corretta, were fans of the Pittsburgh Steelers.

My wife and I are huge fans of the Washington Redskins. At that time, we were season ticket holders. Also, up to that point, we had never taken someone that did not cheer for our team to a game. For the upcoming 2016 season, it was known that the Steelers would travel to Washington for a regular season game. The schedule had not been released yet, but from the annual rotation of games, we knew this would be the case in the fall. As the evening continued,

I told Terri Lee that I wanted to gift the pair of tickets to this game to C.J. and his daughter. She embraced the idea.

We approached C.J. and I told him the news. He called Corretta over to join our conversation and the excitement began to build immediately. It was already evident that they were looking forward to going.

Early into 2016, the Redskins' organization announced that there would be a Guns and Roses concert at FedEx Field. Our season ticket package includes complimentary seats to any event held at the stadium. I didn't have any interest in attending this concert. Generally, in such situations, we would find someone who would appreciate the experience and gift those tickets. A couple of weeks after the organization announced the concert, they followed up with an offer. Anyone receiving complimentary tickets could exchange them for Club Level seating for the first regular season home game. That was a no-brainer. I immediately accepted the offer. A couple of months later, the 2016 season schedule was announced. Wouldn't you know it, but the Steelers vs. Redskins game would be the first one of the season. Terri Lee and I would be attending the game with C.J. and Corretta.

The game was scheduled for Monday, September 12th. It was the first of two Monday Night games scheduled for that day. The plan was for C.J. to preach his service the morning of September 11th. Then, we would pick up C.J. in Bassett that afternoon and the three of us, (Terri Lee, C.J. and myself) would drive to Maryland to his daughter's home. We would then spend the next two nights together, breaking bread, enjoying the game, and being open to whatever else might unfold.

The trip to Maryland was uneventful. We arrived safely in the late evening around 10:00 pm. We were surprised to find that C.J.'s sister, Trevia, and Trevia's husband, Herman, were also at the house to greet us. It was such a warm welcome into Corretta's home.

After a brief visit downstairs, Corretta took us upstairs to a guest room where we would be staying. When we opened the door, we discovered two Redskins' t-shirts laid out on the bed. On the back, each shirt was lettered with the number 5 and the name CLARK. Immediately, I was thinking, "Why did Corretta put Donovan McNabb's number on the t-shirt?" Then, I heard my wife speak up, "Oh, the Clark 5, that's so sweet!" There are five in our immediate family – Terri Lee and me and our three daughters,

Jordan, Caitlin, and Whitney. I had to confess my confusion out loud – and that's when the laughter began. I don't think we stopped laughing until Terri Lee and I were on the interstate heading home two days later.

On Monday morning, I was sitting at the kitchen table. Corretta was working from her laptop at the kitchen counter. I received an email from a woman. I mentioned her in an earlier chapter as her and her husband had traveled to hear me share the testimony of the accident and the court case four separate times. On June 19th, she had shared that the story was having a profound impact on her and her husband. This is the email I received that Monday morning, sitting in the kitchen of C.J.'s daughter:

A while back I told you that God used you and your testimony to prepare my husband's heart and my heart for challenges that we were soon going to face requiring a forgiving heart. It's time for me to tell you my husband's story.

When he was a senior in high school/freshman in college his parents divorced, and his father later remarried. For several years my husband would have absolutely no contact with his father and stepmother whatsoever. When his half-sister was born, he reconnected with them but only for the purpose of being able to see her once in a while. Over the years, and throughout our marriage, he has "softened" a lot toward his dad and stepmother – but there was still resentment and anger that would surface frequently.

You know that his father is dying. This process has been extremely prolonged – and his stepmother told us Saturday when we were there that even their pastor asked him last week what is holding him back; i.e., why is Dad afraid to let go. On the way home, my husband and I were talking about that. We vetted through various answers – then he said something that made me cry: "I wonder if Dad understands that I've forgiven him? I need to let him know that I only have love for both of them now and I've let go of the anger." PURPOSE FULFILLED!

My husband is an extremely private person, and probably won't share this very often. But I wanted you to know how, again, God used you J.T. We didn't know it at the time, but the day we met you and first heard your story – you sensed it. Thank you, my brother and friend, for being who you are and doing God's will!

I was stunned as I read this email. Many, many times since I had begun sharing this story, I have questioned, "Does it really matter? Is it impacting anyone?" When such doubts creep into my consciousness, I receive a message of confirmation like this. Powerful!

Later that afternoon, while the laughs continued through the day, Terri Lee, C.J., Corretta, and I made our way from Corretta's home in suburban Maryland to FedEx Field. It was only about a 15-minute car ride. Before we knew it, we were pulling into our parking space at the stadium. Game Day! I had never taken anyone to a game that wasn't there to cheer for the Redskins. On this day that didn't matter. We had a great time tailgating in the parking lot before entering the stadium. When we got inside, I revealed a special surprise I had waiting for them. I had arranged to provide them with two complimentary pregame field passes. That's right, C.J. and Corretta would get to go down on the perimeter of the field around the Steelers side during pregame warm-ups. Little did I know, but the Redskins organization had a surprise for me, too. They provided Terri Lee and me with passes also.

The excitement for this Monday night game was palpable. It was so much fun being on the sidelines and watching the expressions on the faces of C.J. and Corretta. They were within arms-length of some of the Steeler greats like Antonio Brown and Le'Veon Bell. They watched as Ben Rothlesberger loosened up his throwing arm throwing bullets to his pass catchers.

As we stood just beyond the edge of the field along the sideline at one end zone, my current favorite Redskin, Left Tackle Trent Williams, was walking the perimeter of the field, part of his pregame routine. He stopped to speak with the four of us and have a photograph taken with us. It added to the specialness of the day.

As game time approached, we escorted C.J. and Corretta to their seats on the front row in the back of the end zone at one end of the field. Terri Lee and I made our way to our seats at the Club Level on the opposite end of the field. As a Redskins fan, the game did not go as I would have liked. It mattered not. From the photographs, selfies, and text messages that Corretta was sending us throughout the game, I knew that they were having a big time. From our seats at the club level, I was presented with an opportunity to witness to a man who was sitting beside me. In fact, the 1st quarter concluded almost before we knew there was a game being played. Since that night, Robbie Salem and I have remained in contact through Facebook.

Following breakfast on Tuesday morning, Terri Lee and I said our goodbyes and began the trip back to Southwest Virginia. C.J. had planned to remain with his daughter for the rest of the week and would return home on the weekend. My face was literally sore to the touch from having laughed with such energy for the past couple of days. We each knew that the healing process that had begun almost as soon as the accident had occurred was continuing in earnest. We continued to find a way to love our way through it all.

"And whatsoever ye do in word or deed, do all in the name of the Lord Jesus, giving thanks to God and the Father by him."
Colossians 3:17 (KJV)

CHAPTER 12

PRISON MINISTRY

MARK 16:15 (KJV)

"And he said unto them, Go ye into all the world, and preach the gospel to every creature."

For most of my life, I lived with a callous attitude toward those who found themselves incarcerated. *Look at the choices you made. You did this to yourself*, I would think. When it came to prison facilities, my attitude was always, build them bigger and remove anything that could be construed as a comfort. The idea that I would ever be involved in prison ministry was unfathomable.

Bobby and Pam have a son. Torrey is a highly-intelligent man. He served as a missionary along with his parents in China. He experienced much in terms of helping other people. He was taught the fundamentals of love, compassion, kindness, and forgiveness. But Torrey developed an addiction to drugs. Yet, his parents loved him through it all. They stood alongside him as he made choices driven by his addiction. They desired to be a part of his recovery. Unlike many people who find themselves incarcerated and alone, Torrey had the unconditional love and support of his parents.

Torrey was incarcerated at the New River Valley Regional Jail on August 21st, 2015. He would learn the next day that both of his parents had been killed in a motorcycle accident. I cannot imagine the added torment that has had on him. I have since shared with him that his incarceration at the time of his parent's accident may very well have saved his life. Had he been living with his addiction on the outside when this occurred, we might have lost him, too.

At the time of the accident, I did not have a relationship with him. I lived judgmentally. I had been looking down on Torrey and my brother. *How could they allow this to happen?* I would think with indignation. When the accident occurred, my very being began to be transformed. I began to look at things from a new perspective. It was nearly an overnight transition. I knew that I needed to step into my nephew's life. I knew that if the roles were reversed, my brother would have done it for me in an instant. But how could I do this? How could I go from having no relationship with him to suddenly showing up in his life – not replace his father; but to remind him that he was not alone.

I reached out to his sister, my niece, Robin. I knew that she was being thrust into a role concerning her brother that she had not asked for either. I began to understand that I needed to be there to support them both. I asked Robin to keep me posted about the court dates that Torrey would face. I assured Robin that I did not want to interfere with the process. I just wanted it to be evident that I was there for them. The first court process for which I would be present was a proceeding in federal court. I sat in the gallery just a few rows behind the tables for the prosecution and the defense. Torrey and I were not allowed to speak or have contact, but we saw one another. As other proceedings happened at the state level, I travelled to be present for those as well. It didn't matter whether the proceeding was a mere formality announcing a continuance, or if testimony was being shared, I vowed to be present in the courtroom. I needed Torrey to see that I was there each time. I needed Robin to feel my presence and the love that I was there to share with her and Torrey.

On Thanksgiving Day 2015, we had gathered at Robin's home with her and her family. I took this opportunity to speak with Torrey for just a couple of moments over the telephone. That call was followed up by another on Christmas. In January 2016, Torrey began to call me directly. The question of, "How can I do this (develop a relationship with Torrey)?" was beginning to be answered. It began by simply showing up. By being present in the courtroom, so that he could see evidence that I was there for him. Speaking with him a couple of times on a phone call that was shared with many. Now, having him call me directly – just to speak with me.

Wow! It wasn't so hard. I just needed to set my judgments down and walk in humility, especially in this situation.

In the beginning, he would call me routinely – several times a week. The jail's telephone system limited the calls to 20 minutes. It cost Torrey 25 cents for each minute we spoke. A 20-minute phone call would cost him $5.00. Torrey was fortunate to have money available on his telephone account so that he could call his sister daily and me several times a week. I looked forward to his calls. I cherished the times we got to talk.

After five months, the calls began to reduce in frequency. By the time June arrived, the calls pretty much stopped altogether. I remember feeling sad about that. The way the telephone system was set up, I could not call in to the jail facility to speak with Torrey. He had to initiate the call. For the months of June and July, I maybe spoke with him one or two times. At about 8:00 pm on Monday, August 1st, 2016, I was on Route 220 heading south from Roanoke, VA toward my home in Boones Mill. I was stopped at a traffic light in front of the Outback and Bojangles Restaurants. As I sat there waiting for the light to turn green, I reflected on my relationship with Torrey. I was lamenting the fact that I was no longer talking with him regularly. I wondered why our relationship had fallen off so suddenly. I was missing our conversations and feeling a little sorry for myself. As I sat there, the Holy Ghost admonished me, "What are you doing?! He (Torrey) is the one who needs encouragement. Not you! Write him a letter."

"Write him a letter?" I had never considered that. When I got home and greeted my wife, I immediately fetched a piece of printer paper and wrote a message to my nephew. It was a couple of pages long. I sent it to him in the mail the next morning. For the next 134 straight days, I wrote him a new letter every day. Sometimes it only filled the front of one side of a piece of paper. Other times, it was longer. The length of the letter didn't matter, it was akin to showing up in the courtroom. It served as a reminder that he was not alone. I was walking this journey with him. Within two weeks of writing to him, I began to receive telephone calls from him again. He also started writing me letters. In the beginning, the letters were conversational in nature. As we approached November, I set out a challenge to Torrey. I told him that I wanted any letter that he wrote me to be reflective of what he was thankful for at that time. I would reciprocate and do the same. His November letters began by expressing thankfulness for an exciting World Series and the Cubs eventually winning the title. By the end of the month, Torrey was expressing thankfulness for the example that his parents lived. He shared how he was trying to live their example out in front of others. In subsequent months, we began to share reflections on different books and chapters of the bible. I would send him my perspective on what God was revealing to me and he would do the same. This process continued through the time that he was being transitioned from a regional jail to a state prison.

Torrey was accepted into the dog program at the facility where he is currently located. In this program, he is assigned a dog who is being developed as a service animal. Torrey's responsibility is to work with the animal to complete basic obedience training. Once the dog successfully passes a number of established measures, the dog is then removed from the facility and assigned to an organization outside of the prison for the final training. This program provides Torrey will an outlet and something productive upon which he can focus. It is also a skill set he will retain when he is released from the facility

During a recent trip to the correctional center to visit with Torrey, something was heavy on my heart. Prior to the accident, I did not have

much of a relationship with him. In fact, I did not have much of a relationship with anyone. God had laid something on my heart to share with Torrey that day. The impact of what I said to him was evident in the look on his face as he heard me. Tears welled up in his eyes and a lump formed in his throat. Further evidence of the impact was revealed when I received an electronic message from him not more than 20 minutes after I had left the prison facility.

I told him that when I showed up in the courtroom for one of his proceedings for the first time, just a few weeks after his parent's accident, I did so because I knew that his dad would have done the same for my family if the circumstances were reversed. I told him that while the renewing of our relationship may have started that way, that is not why it would continue. I said, "I don't come to visit you now because your dad would have done the same for one of our daughters. I don't come to visit you because I owe your dad. No. The reason I come to visit you is that I love you. I come because of the relationship that we have developed. I come to visit you to encourage you. I visit to minister to you. I come to remind you that you are not forgotten, and you are not alone."

Helping, comforting, and ministering to a family member is a far cry from what I would call a prison ministry. That is not to minimize or discourage an individual from being connected to someone who is incarcerated. For me, it turns out that it was merely the beginning. As I spoke with Torrey, he would share some of the things that we had discussed, or about which I would write, with other inmates. Before long, other men began reaching out to me through letters and telephone calls.

People would often ask me about our ministry, *My Brothers' Crossing*. They wanted to know what kinds of ministry we got involved. I was surprised at how involved we had become in prison ministry and outreach. Our ministry does not have a budget of which to speak. Whatever limited funding we receive is mostly in the form of love offerings for speaking engagements. The money would immediately be used to help another person.

One man to whom I would be connected through my nephew is named Kelsey. As of this time, he has transitioned from the regional jail, to a state receiving unit, to one prison facility, and has just been moved to another prison. He and I talk regularly. We have shared scriptures back and forth. Through our ministry, we have helped him with limited commissary support. Most of all, my wife and I have sought to bring hope to his life. We wanted to encourage him. We wanted him to study, learn, and know the gospel.

Kelsey has been captivated by the testimony that I have been sharing. I sent him copies of the newspaper articles as they appeared. He ended up sharing this information with others with whom he was incarcerated. Wherever his travels would take him through the system, he would share our story and our ministry contact information. As a result, we became connected to more and more men who wanted to connect with us from prison. Kelsey would say, "I am planting chapters of *My Brothers' Crossing* wherever I go."

At the first state prison facility where Kelsey was assigned after completing the intake/receiving process, he confessed that he was not prepared for what he was encountering. The environment was much worse than he had imagined. He called me nearly every day. Unlike the regional jail where 20-minute telephone calls cost five dollars, at the state prisons, the same telephone call cost only 87 cents. Each time we spoke, Kelsey would share the impact being able to speak with my wife and me by telephone and how the encouragement he received was helping him in his transition.

Since the beginning of our relationship, Kelsey had worked on creating art. He would sometimes mail me his artwork as he completed it. I have a limited imagination and have great difficulty drawing a straight line with two hands and a ruler. I was fascinated by the art he created. When he was moved to the first state prison following intake/receiving, Kelsey met a man named Randy. He introduced Randy to my wife and me. Not too long after being assigned to this prison facility, Kelsey was moved to a different pod at the same prison compound. Kelsey and Randy would not have contact again so long as they remained at different pods. Randy was also an artist with skill at a much higher level than Kelsey. Don't get me wrong, Kelsey could produce stuff that I would never be able to even imagine. Randy was just that much more talented.

Prior to them being separated within the prison compound, Randy had started an art piece that would be a gift for Kelsey's mother for her birthday. Since they were now separated, Randy had no way of getting it to Kelsey's mom. They were able to maintain a connection through our ministry, so Randy mailed the artwork to us. When it arrived, my wife and I agreed that it needed to be matted and framed before shipping to

Kelsey's mother. From the frame shop to the shipping company, there was an opportunity to minister to everyone with whom we had contact. In mid-September 2017, we shipped a matted and framed picture of a scene featuring a hummingbird to the address provided to me by Kelsey. In advance of shipping it, we had also received a card in the mail from Kelsey that he wanted us to include with it. We arranged to have the shipping done in such a way that it appeared it was Kelsey who had sent it.

On Thursday, September 21st, I received a telephone call from Kelsey. He had just gotten off the telephone with his mom and dad. Through tears, he shared with me the joy that his mom expressed in receiving his gift and card. She had no idea it was coming. Then Kelsey said something to me that overwhelmed me. He said, "For the first time in over 30 years, I heard my dad say, 'I love you.'" I was brought to tears. What I had imagined was just a simple, yet beautiful piece of artwork opened doors for me to share the gospel with many other people. What had intended to be a gesture of love between Kelsey and his mom, brought down a wall between Kelsey and his father.

Kelsey and I continue to talk. My wife and I continue to minister to and encourage him. We have met his brother and sister-in-law and his nieces as they traveled to hear me on one of the occasions where I was speaking. As of this time, we are trying to work it out to transport his parents to the facility where he is currently imprisoned for a visitation.

I met another man at the regional jail where my nephew had been housed. We began to have conversations in 2016 and continued these through the time he was released in November 2017. During a telephone conversation in July 2017, this man shared with me about his son's 5th birthday that was approaching in a couple of days. As we talked, I was moved to inquire as to his son's interests. The man told me he liked trains. After our telephone call concluded, I placed an order through Amazon for a train set and a book about trains to be shipped to the young fellow at his grandparents' home. I rationalized that it was not the boy's fault that his father was not available to be with him on his birthday. Once again, I arranged for this gift to be shipped as though the imprisoned man sent it.

The next month, this man sent me a letter. The letter included a poem. This man, who I had not yet met in person, had penned a poem about our ministry. He wrote the poem as if I wrote it. He wrote it using my words.

My Brothers' Crossing
by James Linville

The Lord works in mysterious ways
And more than that on that fateful day.

When God called home my brother and his wife,
God brought another brother into my life.

They say accidents happen any time, any place.
Some call it destiny. Others call it fate.

Like I never planned on forgiving this man;
Much less call him brother, but that was God's plan.

Now I give God my all; gave my life over to him;
And pray for the sick; make prisoners my friends.

So, when I open my eyes and start each new day,
I give it back to God. I want HIS WILL, HIS WAY!

Everything that I do, to God it's my offering.
And what once made my heart bitter is now
My Brothers' Crossing.

As for Randy, I am working to get his artwork noticed. His artwork is of a caliber that I think there might be interest at another level than just the casual observer. Randy is greatly encouraged to know that something that God creates through him brings a smile, brings joy to another human being. It is powerful to operate a ministry that gives other people an opportunity to be God's messengers.

I estimate that I am now in communication with more than two dozen inmates, and in some cases, their families. Truthfully, it started without me even realizing what was happening. I did not have a master plan. But as it turns out, my Master has had a plan all along. A work that began in my brother was now being continued through me.

I have just been accepted into a program being offered at the local jail in our community. It is a program called "Bridging the Gap" that our sheriff has begun. I will lead a small group of men in a weekly devotional on Wednesday mornings. It is just another opportunity to touch and impact lives.

Early on, I wondered how my judgments and biases would impact my ability to relate to the men in these situations. While I have never been physically incarcerated in a prison facility, I was spiritually imprisoned for decades. I also began to understand that some of the choices I had made in my life were maybe only a step or two away from ending up in this very situation.

I don't ask these men why they have been incarcerated. If they choose to freely share this information, I don't stop them either. I just don't want my knowledge of their circumstance to be a barrier to me being able to minister to them. Thus far, I have not encountered a single individual who has said that he is wrongfully imprisoned. Each person to whom we have ministered has acknowledged their mistakes and wants to atone for them.

The God I serve is a God of second opportunities. Sometimes, we are blessed to have multiple opportunities. He is waiting with open arms to receive us. For many, like me, it has taken many missed opportunities to find that one circumstance that brought me to my knees. Through this aspect of our ministry, we want to encourage and pour hope into the lives of others. We want to let them know there is another way. They can make a different choice.

"Then will I teach transgressors thy ways; and sinners shall be converted unto thee."
Psalm 51:13 (KJV)

CHAPTER 13

ARE YOU AVAILABLE TO ATTEND THE NFL DRAFT?

Joshua 1:9 (KJV)

"Have not I commanded thee? Be strong and of a good courage; be not afraid, neither be thou dismayed: for the LORD thy God is with thee whithersoever thou goest."

In March 2017, I had arrived home from work as my wife was preparing to leave for her volunteer EMS shift. It was a Thursday evening a little before 6:00 pm, and I was on our home landline speaking with our youngest daughter who lived in Northern Virginia. As we talked, I noticed an incoming phone call on my cell phone. Not wanting to interrupt the call I was already on to talk with someone else, I let it go to voicemail. I asked my daughter to hold for just a moment while I played the recorded message. After listening to the message, I asked my daughter, "Did you just hear that?" She replied, "No. I could hear someone speaking but I couldn't hear what they were saying." I exclaimed, "I think I just got invited to the NFL Draft!" I told her, "I love you, honey; but, I am going to have to call you back." The call was from a staff member of the Washington Redskins. They were notifying me that I had been randomly selected to be the team's representative for the 2017 NFL Draft in Philadelphia April 26th – April 30th. The message instructed me to contact the representative to let them know if I would be able to clear my calendar to attend.

When I called her back, she filled me in on all the details of the trip and the experience. Amongst other activities, she informed me that I would present the jersey to the NFL Commissioner that would be given to the #1 draft pick of the Washington Redskins. I could not believe what I was hearing. Two days prior, my wife and I had been watching the movie, *Draft Day*, starring Kevin Costner. She asked me, "Who decides who gets to attend the draft?" Two days later we were informed that we would be on our way.

I have been a lifelong Redskins fan. This would be the experience of a lifetime. I could not wrap my mind around it. I was so excited about the opportunity. Yet, just one week prior to the flight I was having second thoughts about going. I was considering having my wife take one of our daughters with her instead of me.

Back in February, C.J. Martin, Mike Price, and I had met for breakfast. We were getting together that morning because we were scheduled to record a TV show that T.R.A.S.H. Ministry produced on a local cable television station each week. This was the first time that C.J. and I would be joining Mike. When we finished breakfast, Mike suggested we stop by his church. He wanted to show some of the enhancements that he had recently made there. Mike gave C.J. and me a tour and highlighted some of the improvements. Before leaving to drive to the studio, Mike told us he had one more thing to show C.J. He went into his office and returned with an instrument case. I could see from the expression on Mike's face that something special was about to happen.

Mike laid the instrument case on a long plastic table. He released the latches that held it closed and flung open the hinged top. He told C.J., "This is a 1972 Fender Bass Guitar. This belonged to my daddy. I just purchased it from my brother. The Holy Ghost just told me to give it to you." C.J. immediately responded, "I cannot take that from you." Mike insisted, "You have no choice. The Holy Ghost told me to give it to you. I am treating this instrument like an idol. You are going to play it to glorify God." With that, the instrument exchanged hands.

"How does this part of the story connect to the NFL Draft?" I am glad you asked.

Every day from that day through mid-April, C.J. spent time and money refurbishing the bass guitar that Mike had gifted to him. C.J. wanted to do this in honor of the brotherhood they shared.

Chapter 13: *Are you available to attend the NFL Draft?*

Mike was asked by the Piedmont Community Services Board to host a Recovery Service. These services are used to celebrate the efforts of former addicts as they continued their walk in deliverance and healing. These services are often used to encourage another who is battling a similar issue. The service was scheduled for Friday, April 28th. C.J.'s church, House of Purpose, was committed to also being in attendance for this special service. Mike invited C.J. to play bass in T.R.A.S.H. Ministry's band, Recycled, for this service. Unbeknownst to Mike, C.J. was intending to bring out the refurbished bass for the first time.

It is challenging for the three of us to get together. Anytime that we can, it is always a special time. I did not want to miss that night, but the service was scheduled for the Friday night while my wife and I would be in Philadelphia.

On Wednesday, April 19th, one week prior to flying to Philadelphia, I was in prayer. I was seeking God as to what I should do about the service versus the trip. I heard God say, "You are to go on this trip. You are to enjoy this time with your wife. Don't worry about the service. I have something for you there (in Philadelphia)." That settled it. But, it also changed my perspective on the trip. While I was looking forward to what I would experience as part of the NFL Draft, I went expecting to find what God had for me there.

We arrived in Philadelphia and were transported to the hotel where we would be staying for the next few days. After checking into our room, my wife and I went to the designated room to check-in with the NFL officials. Each team in the league had selected an individual to be their team's representative and each person selected could bring one guest. There were more than 60 of us in attendance.

The first night, we would attend a reception and receive an orientation as to what the next several days would look like. As part of the reception, we participated in a segment of "You Make the Call?" This was an interactive experience where several individuals were invited to review plays from the previous season that resulted in Replay Review. The Director of Officials for the NFL facilitated this segment and the conversations that followed.

The next morning began with breakfast. We were assigned seats by division. So, as representatives of the Washington Redskins, we were seated with the team representatives from the Philadelphia Eagles, New

York Giants, and Dallas Cowboys. As we ate breakfast, we listened to a panel discussion featuring NFL great and former Philadelphia Eagle quarterback, Ron Jaworski, current NFL Commissioner, Roger Goodell, and current Carolina Panther linebacker, Thomas Davis. Following their comments, we were each invited to ask a question. I used to be such an introvert. I would never want to take an opportunity like this. But I was emboldened and threw my hand in the air. An NFL representative brought a microphone to me. My question was for Roger Goodell. To understand the basis for my question, you have to know that he is routinely and soundly booed as he takes the stage for the draft. I asked him, "Being the team representative for the Washington Redskins and being in the city of one of our division rivals, the Philadelphia Eagles, what advice would you give me to deal with the chorus of boos and the reception that I will get when I step onto the stage tonight to present you the jersey." The room erupted in laughter. Ron Jaworski retorted, "Oh, you will be booed!" Roger Goodell added, "Managing your expectations is a good start."

From there, we were transported to the draft venue. An outdoor venue was created featuring the famous Rocky steps. We were provided a walk-thru of what the evening would look like. We learned how the jerseys were prepared in the moments after receiving word of the team's draft selection. We practiced walking out to present the jersey to the commissioner.

Afterwards, we were transported to another hotel. At this hotel, we were treated to a buffet lunch and another panel discussion featuring four Walter Payton Man-of-the-Year award winners. These included Charles Davis, DeMarcus Ware, Warrick Dunn, and Thomas Davis. Once again as we ate, these men spoke about their NFL careers. At the conclusion of their remarks, the audience was invited to ask questions. The attendance for this gathering was substantially larger than that at breakfast. Other NFL officials and guests were included. Again, I was moved to ask them a question. I raised my hand and a microphone was delivered to me. I stood up and introduced my wife and I asked a question about their faith. I asked, "Each of you spoke about adversity that you faced in your personal life and your playing careers. Can you talk about how your faith helped you in those situations?" In a split second, the conversation switched from talking about football to having these giants of their craft speaking about Jesus Christ.

Chapter 13: *Are you available to attend the NFL Draft?*

Thursday evening, we were transported back to the draft venue from our hotel. Following a brief reception backstage, each team representative and their guest would walk the red carpet carrying the designated draft day ball cap for their team. We would be seated in the first three rows in front of the stage. As the first round of the draft unfolded, the team representative would be escorted backstage to the jersey room where we would await the selection. The pick for the Washington Redskins was reported to the jersey room. Jonathon Allen, defensive tackle from Alabama, was the Redskins' selection. The jersey was prepared and handed to me. Once the commissioner made the announcement, I would walk across the stage from right to left to present it. I was prepared for a noisy reception. The one I received wasn't nearly what I was expecting. The Commissioner commented, "You got a pretty good reception. You must like that pick. He should help your defense." We took a photo together and then I exited. Backstage, an NFL staffer used her smart phone to record a one-take segment where she asked me to describe my day. I was overwhelmed. What an experience.

On Friday, we had most of the day to ourselves. At one point, my wife asked if I would walk up to the drug store to get something for her. We had seen the store during one of our trips on the bus back from the draft venue, so I had an idea where it was. As I left the hotel, I walked down the sidewalk in the direction I remember seeing the drug store. I crossed over a street and started down the next block. As I continued to walk, I heard on my spirit, "Go back and give that man confirmation." As I looked back over my shoulder, I saw a black man standing on the street corner. He was a little animated and he was speaking about Jesus Christ. I apparently had walked past him only a few minutes before, completely oblivious. I turned around and walked back to him. As I approached him, I engaged him in conversation. He told me his name was Danny and that he was homeless. I explained that the Holy Ghost had convicted me to come back and give him confirmation as to the truth he was speaking. I asked him to share his story with me. I then shared my story with him. We hugged. I asked him if he could tell me where the drugstore was located. As it turns out, he was standing ten feet away from the entrance.

I left Danny and went inside to make the purchase. As I was leaving, I was walking toward an ATM machine. I was moved to withdraw $200. I went back outside the store and I handed the money, plus a ministry card with my name and phone number on it to Danny. We took a picture together and I returned to the hotel.

It was getting close to time to go and I needed to return to the drugstore to make another purchase. It seemed that everyone staying at this hotel was there for the NFL Draft. As I exited our room on the sixth floor to go to the elevator, a man, Will, and a woman, Beth, exited another room on the same floor. We walked to the elevator together. Will asked me about all of the excitement and about the draft. He and his sister were in Philadelphia for their nephew's lacrosse tournament. As we made our way down on the elevator and walked toward the hotel lobby, Will said, "That's quite a story." To which I replied, "Oh, if you think that's quite a story, boy do I have one to tell you." The three of us stood in the hotel lobby as I shared the story of my brother's accident and the courtroom scene. Tears had welled up in their eyes by the time we had parted company.

When I arrived back at the hotel a few minutes later, I was moved to enter the bar and restaurant attached to the hotel. There, sitting at the corner of the bar, was Will and Beth. I stepped into the corner between the two of them and he said, "Boy am I glad to see you. We cannot stop talking about what you told us." I took that as an invitation to share more of the story with them both. As I wound down the story, he looked at me and said, "My pastor is going to want to hear this story. I am a member of the oldest African-American church in Washington, D.C. You need to come and share this with our church." He went on to say, this story needs to be made into a movie. He informed me that he used to work in the film industry and that he might be able to make something happen. While nothing has happened in terms of creating a movie from this story, I did receive an invitation to speak at Mt. Zion United Methodist Church in Washington, D.C. just seven weeks later.

Later that afternoon, we would be transported from the hotel back to the draft venue for rounds two and three that evening. I was excited about this evening's rounds as there was a good chance that a man from our community would be selected in the second or third round. Terrell Basham played high school football at Franklin County High School in Virginia. He graduated with one of our daughters. I watched from the sideline as a member of the chain crew during his entire high school career. The anticipation of hearing his name announced was exciting. He was selected in the third round by the Indianapolis Colts.

On the morning of third day of the draft, I received a communication from the Washington Redskins. They wanted to know if we intended to attend the draft on this day. They wanted to know if we would be willing to make the announcement of the team's selection in the sixth round. Absolutely! My wife and I then began to consider – I hope we can pronounce the man's name. I was reflecting on two things. I hoped that whomever we announced would have an impact on the team, and I also hoped that we would get to announce a name that we could pronounce. Robert Davis, a wide receiver from Georgia State, was the draft pick.

On our way home on Sunday, I reflected on what God had for me in Philadelphia. Was it a contact with the NFL? Was it the interaction with Danny? Was it the encounter with Will and his sister? Was it something that was not yet revealed to me? As I thought about all of that, I reflected that it was parts of each of those and more.

"My son, if thou be surety for thy friend, if thou hast stricken thy hand with a stranger, Thou art snared with the words of thy mouth, thou art taken with the words of thy mouth. Do this now, my son, and deliver thyself, when thou art come into the hand of thy friend; go, humble thyself, and make sure thy friend."
Proverbs 6:1-3 (KJV)

CHAPTER 14

ANSWERING THE CALL

2 John 1:6 (KJV)

"And this is love, that we walk after his commandments. This is the commandment, That, as ye have heard from the beginning, ye should walk in it."

On August 2nd, 2017, Mike Price and his wife Stephanie, and C.J. Martin and his wife, Fernanda, and I had gathered for a meal at House of Purpose to discuss the final plans for a youth event we were organizing to be called Youth Arise 2017. It was scheduled for Saturday, August 26th. Following our meeting, and just before Bible study was to begin, C.J. looked at me and asked, "Have you got the call?" I knew what he was asking, and a smile spread across my face. He said, "Let's get you scheduled to have your Initial Sermon. This will complete your ordination process." He explained it to me this way. "You are already doing the work. You are stepping into the lives of other people. You are ministering to those in need. You are already speaking in churches. This will just formalize it all." He suggested August 27th for the service.

I asked him who he would recommend I speak with leading up to this day. He recommended a man named Johnell Manns, an Elder at House of Purpose. Elder Manns and I had the opportunity to talk. He told me how proud he was of the work that I was doing since the accident had happened. He talked to me about the impact I was having on the House of Purpose

Ministry. We discussed my views and he encouraged me to continue to study God's Word. He challenged me to remain humble and obedient as I did God's will.

For the Friday before the youth event and Initial Sermon, I arranged a prayer breakfast. Mike Price offered to host it at T.R.A.S.H. Ministry. I invited many of the church leaders who had opened their hearts to me over the prior two years. I wanted a time of prayer and a time of reflection. I wanted each of them to know and hear from me the impact they had on me as I developed and grew in ministry. Some could not make it. Many did. I was lifted by the experience of it.

On my drive home following this breakfast, I was reminded of an audio cassette that my mom had given to me. It was a recording of a sermon Bobby preached prior to heading to China. When I arrived home, I searched and found the cassette tape and listened to it. As I listened, I thought, this is just the introduction I would have spoken at my Initial Sermon. It dawned on me that while many people at House of Purpose had seen photographs of my brother and heard stories of my brother, none had heard his voice. I thought, I will transfer the first part of his sermon, the introduction, from the cassette to my iPhone and use this for my introduction.

The title of my message was, "It's Your Race." It was to be a perspective that our faith walks are just that, ours. It is a personal relationship and experience between us and our Savior. It is not anything anyone else can do for us. It is ours alone to do. We each have a course to run. It's personal.

That Sunday arrived. I drove to House of Purpose for the regular 11:00 am service. As I entered the sanctuary, my ministry phone rang with a Philadelphia phone number. I did not recognize the number. Normally, I would just let it go to voicemail. In this instance, however, I stepped outside and answered it. From the other end, I heard, "J.T. This is Danny. Do you remember me?" I was floored. I responded, "Of course I remember you, Danny. I talk about you wherever I go." He proceeded to tell me that when he woke up that morning, the Holy Spirit laid it on him to call and give me a word of encouragement. I asked him if he knew what today was. He said no. He just knew that before he could do anything else, he had to call me to encourage me. I explained that I was getting ready to deliver my Initial Sermon and I could sure use the encouragement. A man I had only met once before in April was calling me one day short of four months to the day that I had met him. He went on to tell me that he was no longer homeless. Obviously, I was going to work this telephone conversation into the message I would share in just a couple of hours.

In addition to my House of Purpose family who had returned to the church for the service, my wife, my mom, my sister, and my youngest and eldest daughter and her husband had come to bear witness to this service.

The time arrived for the service to start. A special program had been developed for the afternoon's service. The House of Purpose worship team would lead us in songs and C.J. Martin and Mike Price would make some comments. Then, it would be my turn. As the worship team finished their selection, C.J. stepped to the pulpit and asked the worship team to sing one more song. He explained that they had a special surprise for me and they needed just a few more minutes for it to arrive.

About two-thirds of the way through the song, the front door of the church opened, and two tall, thin black men entered. I recognized one of them instantly. My knees nearly buckled as I thought I would drop to the floor. It was Billy Cogman, the husband of the pastor of the church in Washington, D.C. and his brother. This man, whom I had met just ten weeks before, and his brother had made a five-hour trip, one-way, just to bear witness to my Initial Sermon.

At the conclusion of the message that I shared, C.J. asked if anyone in attendance had any remarks to share in reflection. Several people took the opportunity to speak. My mother shared about how my brother and I pursued the same vocations, except ministry. Now, I was doing that also. My sister spoke expressing her pride in what I was doing with my life. She said she never knew I could speak like that. Each of my daughters who were there shared that they never saw this coming for their father. They, too, were proud, and excited to see this change in my life.

Billy would tell that had he not been able to make the trip, there were 14 others who were ready to travel in his place. They made a ten-hour round trip just to hear my Initial Sermon. Billy explained that I had such an impact on their congregation when I was up there to serve and speak a few weeks prior, they were compelled to send a delegation for this service.

Following these remarks, C.J. completed the ordination process. He asked me to affirm my beliefs in Jesus Christ, the Holy Bible, and my commitment to serve. With my responses in agreement, he and Elder

Manns prayed over my wife and me. A framed Certificate of License and a framed Certificate of Ordination were presented to me. I was now officially able to preach, perform marriages, administer the Sacraments, and to direct the other functions of the ministry.

> *"Let nothing be done through strife or vainglory; but in lowliness of mind let each esteem other better than themselves."*
> *Philippians 2:3 (KJV)*

CHAPTER 15

A MIRACLE HEALING

LUKE 9:11 (KJV)

"And the people, when they knew it, followed him: and he received them, and spake unto them of the kingdom of God, and healed them that had need of healing."

On Wednesday, December 20th, 2017, I received a text message from a man named Jack. I enjoyed a special friendship with Jack. We both enjoyed our food and we both loved the Washington Redskins. I consider myself a pretty big sports fan in general. Jack is on a whole other level than me. On this day, he had sent me a message asking if I could meet with him. The message did not seem to be sent in distress or with any urgency. I replied that I would catch up with him on my way through Boones Mill after I finished one other meeting. After the one meeting had concluded, I tried to reach Jack, to no avail. Again, his text message did not seem to be anything out of the ordinary, so I did not think much about it when I could not reach him. I didn't think much about it when I didn't hear back from him.

On Saturday morning, December 23rd about 1:30 am, I received a Facebook Messenger message from Holly. She messaged me to say that since Jack had tried to reach out to me, he would probably want me to know. She said he was in critical condition in the Neuro Intensive Care Unit at Carilion Medical Center (CMC). She explained that he was on a ventilator, his liver was failing, and the prognosis was not good. I was in shock at hearing the news.

Later that morning, I traveled to CMC to visit Holly and Jack. I wanted to show my support and to pray for both of them and the entirety of the circumstances. I also wanted to read some bible verses. I was not prepared to see Jack in this condition. He did not look good. He was bloated, and his skin was jaundiced. He was in a bad situation. C.J. Martin and I had talked when I was on my way to visit Jack. He had encouraged me to speak to Jack just as though he was awake and alert. He encouraged me to speak boldly over his life and to read scripture, knowing that God can deliver the message to Jack's spirit. Pastor Andrew Columbia offered the same counsel.

I made two trips to see Jack on Saturday, Sunday, and Monday, which was Christmas Day. I called on the prayer warriors I knew from the many churches I had visited. I asked for people to fervently pray on Jack's behalf. Holly shared that the news did not look good. She was informed at one point that Jack needed a new liver, but that he was not a good candidate for a transplant. Many, many people prayed and moved in support of both Holly and Jack. I could not make it to visit daily, but many did. It seemed as though Holly never left Jack's side.

When I would visit, I would pray. I would read scriptures. I would lay hands on Jack's sickened body and ask for healing and recovery. I followed the counsel offered by pastors C.J. Martin and Andrew Columbia. Eventually, after being hospitalized at CMC for weeks, Jack improved enough that he became eligible for a liver transplant at Johns Hopkins University.

Jack is continuing to be treated post-transplant. He is doing well. He has returned to work and is experiencing a life transformation.

I saw the evidence of the power of prayer in this situation. A community of believers poured prayer, love, hope, and faith over the lives of Holly and Jack. In fact, Holly poured herself into his life, seemingly never leaving his side through it all. It was something to witness God move through this situation.

> *"How God anointed Jesus of Nazareth with the Holy Ghost and with power: who went about doing good, and healing all that were oppressed of the devil; for God was with him."*
> *Acts 10:38 (KJV)*

CHAPTER 16

J.T. WASN'T ALWAYS THIS WAY

BY: TERRI LEE CLARK

EPHESIANS 2:8 (KJV)

"For by grace are ye saved through faith; and that not of yourselves:
it is the gift of God."

To give everyone a bit of history about myself, I grew up in a Christian home — going to church, praying, and having a very strong belief in God. But I didn't know what was to come in my life at a young age and how my faith in God would be tested. At 19 years old, I married my high school sweetheart, John Claybrook Richards. We had dated for 3½ years before getting married. Our marriage started off with both of us working. Additionally, I was attending college, and volunteered as a firefighter and an EMT at our local fire and rescue department. I was also in the process of becoming a paramedic with dreams of eventually becoming a physician. My faith was tested just sixteen months into our marriage when my husband was killed. There was an event that had occurred just over a month prior to my husband's death that, at the time, seemed to be what led to his death.

In the year after his death, I tried to wrap my head around all that had happened during the past year and how my life had been turned upside down in a matter of seconds. My dream of becoming a physician didn't seem so important any longer. I no longer had my husband with whom to share this plan for a family and all that we would do. After all, I couldn't save his life, so how could I possibly save the lives of others? In February, just about thirteen months after my husband's death, I met John Thomas (J.T.) Clark, who would become my husband just six months after we met. Many thought it was too soon after my first husband's death, but I knew in my heart that God had sent this man to me. Little did I know that not only did God send him to me, but he placed me in J.T.'s life. He placed me there beside him through what to that point, had been a battle with severe depression for the previous 7 years.

During the first twenty-three years of our marriage, J.T. dealt with severe depression and suicidal ideation, including suicide attempts. I spent what seemed like every waking moment in prayer asking God to heal him, laying hands on him as he slept, and praying over him. I wrote letters to God that were placed in my Bible which quickly filled up, later to be stored in a crate.

Writing letters to God doesn't sound like something that would be of help. For me, the physical act of writing letters to God was my way of casting my burdens upon Him. Going to God through my writing to give up J.T.'s depression, my doubts, my fears, and all that goes along with it, was my way of crying out to Him. Living with a spouse whom you love with all of your heart and hearing him say every day, 'I don't want to live. I just want to be dead!' is extremely difficult. These are very difficult words to hear from anyone, but from your husband, best friend, and father of your children, it is especially difficult. It almost seemed as though in one breath he would tell me how much he loved me and adored me and our three beautiful daughters and in the next breath, he was consumed by his desire to be dead. When I would write these letters to God, I felt a weight lifted from me because I knew I couldn't heal J.T. on my own. I needed to give this to God. It didn't mean that I no longer needed to pray. I would continue to pray. But, I had given this over to God and that's what He wants us to do. He's just waiting for His children to cry out to Him.

During those years of depression, we became parents to three beautiful daughters. Jordan Carrissa was born on November 15th, 1992. Caitlin Alexandra was born on November 20th, 1993. And Whitney Leann came into this world on December 11th, 1994. Needless to say, I had a lot on my plate with three children all just under 3 ½ years old. I was busy being a mother, wife, paramedic, and caretaker for my husband.

J.T. was able to function at work; he was able to hide the signs of his deep depression. When he came home at night, he was worn out from having to put on a facade for those he would come into contact with throughout the day. For much of this time, he worked as a director of facilities management at three different hospitals. In his role as a department director, he had many people who worked for him in his departments. They counted on him for leadership and guidance. He carried a great deal of stress as he tried to cope with his mental health challenges. He wanted to provide for his family and did not want others to know about his challenges. We did our best to maintain it as a family secret. Once upon a time, having depression or any other mental health condition placed a label on people. A stigma was attached. These individuals can be made to feel that they don't fit in; they don't belong. Often, it is simply something about how their brains are wired or a chemical imbalance, but not always.

One large misconception is that depression is just a mental illness. Depression not only affects the way we feel emotionally, but it also affects the entire body such as: muscle and joint pain, chest pain, digestive problems, debilitating exhaustion and fatigue to the point where it becomes physically impossible to get out of bed. It causes problems with sleep, which J.T. dealt with on a regular basis. Headaches, migraines, changes in appetite, weight gain, and weight loss are all among the host of physical symptoms that can be a part of depression.

The treatment most often given by physicians is to place their patients on antidepressants. Counseling, group therapy, and other modalities are often used in treatment as well. It is the belief of some that if our God has the ability to heal, then people suffering from depression don't need to be on medication for it. This is not true. The medications given to those with depression serve a purpose to "tweak" the chemicals your nerve cell network uses to communicate, making them work more efficiently. Again, you can see where another "label" is often placed on those who are taking medication to help with the symptoms of depression.

God has given those who work in the pharmaceutical industry the ability to make a chemical compound that helps produce the chemical changes necessary for the nerve cells to interact appropriately. These are just a few examples of what J.T. had to deal with during his 30-year long battle with depression and suicidal ideation. I can only begin to imagine the additional stress that this places on a person who is already feeling overwhelmed with what must feel like an unending uphill battle with no signs of light.

The level of depression I felt after the tragic death of my first husband was from the grief I felt and from Post-Traumatic Stress Disorder from being the first one the scene and witnessing his death. My depression was something that with time and going through the stages of grief would eventually diminish. That is not to say that his death no longer saddens me, but I came to terms with his death through my faith in Jesus, knowing that I would one day see him again because he was saved and was promised eternal life by our Father in heaven.

As it concerned J.T.'s suicidal ideation, I became convinced that it was just Satan getting into his mind and his thinking. I believe the enemy was whispering to him telling him that he was a burden on his family and friends. He felt as though he had no purpose here on earth. These are all the lies Satan tells and the closer those battling depression pull towards God; the harder Satan comes at them trying to pull them away from God. Satan shows them that God has let them down and if our God is a God who has the ability to heal, then why isn't He healing you and why are you having to continue going through this torment? Satan can show us things we can see, such as the mental anguish you are going through, the battle to keep your job, the effort to keep it together and manage a family. He shows you your weaknesses and knows that your faith in God isn't something that can be seen, but rather faith is confidence in what we hope for and evidence of what we do not see.

I'm sure as you're reading this you're wondering what this has to do with this story. The place that this has in this story, that many people don't know, is that during the first twenty-three years of our marriage I was pretty much dragging J.T. to church with our daughters and myself, but he was just physically there. He wasn't being filled with the spirit of God because he was in so much mental pain he wasn't in a place where he could receive God's grace. He tried over and over during those years to push me away, to get me to leave him and take our daughters. Although he would tell me how much he loved me and our daughters, he felt that he was a burden on me and our family and we would be better off without him. I knew that if I left and took our daughters, then he would take his life because he would have no reason to live. I wasn't about to let that happen.

I loved J.T. with all of my heart and knew that he loved me just as much, but he felt unworthy because of the lies that Satan was putting into his head. There were so many people who told me that I should take our daughters and leave J.T. I heard from many people that I shouldn't be in a marriage with someone who was putting so much stress on me. Being a paramedic, I dealt with more victims of suicide than I care to remember. Every day I wondered if that day would be the day that I would find a State Trooper or a Deputy at my door giving me the news that my husband had succeeded in taking his life.

This caused much mental anguish for me. As a paramedic, I was accustomed to saving the lives of those who wanted to live. Although many of my patients were Christians and believed in eternal life, they still were not ready to go home to be with the Lord. They still had things they wanted to do here on earth with their loved ones. It was hard knowing I could make a difference in the life of a stranger but couldn't change how my husband perceived himself and his desire to be dead.

If I would have walked out with our daughters and left J.T., he most certainly would have taken his life and Satan would have won. J.T. wouldn't have been here for the things that God had planned for his life. He wouldn't have been here to move in forgiveness towards Mr. Martin, to spread the gospel of Christ Jesus to so many people, especially to those to whom others don't want to minister. He wouldn't have been here for the two of us to start our ministry. We would have missed out on travel from church to church and other venues telling the story. A story of how this horrible tragedy has brought together groups of people from very different walks of life that society says shouldn't be worshiping together, celebrating God's grace and mercy together, or sitting down for casual conversation and a meal together.

You see, I loved J.T. and I knew that Satan was at the root of my husband's efforts to push me away. I knew the love J.T. had for me. I knew how Satan worked and how he could twist things around and tell lies to pull a person away from God. But God had bigger plans for J.T. and for me, but we had to go on this journey for J.T. to receive his healing.

Some may ask, "Why would God have let J.T. suffer for so very long?" I think it boils down to this. J.T. had to learn about forgiveness. In fact, the breakthrough in his mental health battle came in 2009. He had to move in forgiveness toward a situation which had occurred in his childhood. When he experienced this breakthrough, it was as if someone threw a switch. He no longer wanted to be dead. In fact, he wanted to live. Because of this breakthrough in forgiveness, he has been moved to forgive in many other situations since that time.

I had a strong relationship with God. It was strengthened further and made more intimate because of all that I was going through. I loved a man who suffered so deeply. I had doubts as to whether he would return home at the end of each day. This caused me to place even greater faith in my Lord and Savior. I had three beautiful daughters that I was raising and lived with the constant thought that at such a young age they may lose their father by a choice that he had made and not by an accident or a medical problem. How would I explain that to them? In my experience of dealing with the family members of a victim of suicide, the parents, spouse, and children blame themselves for not seeing the signs or for knowing that their loved one suffered from depression. They blamed themselves for not trying hard enough to get them the help they needed. I knew I could tell our daughters that I did everything I could to get him medical help and spiritual counseling, and I showed him love even when he felt like he was unlovable and not deserving of being loved. These things grew my relationship with God to a level that was beyond anything I could have ever imagined.

Our God isn't a God who punishes us or causes us physical or mental pain. Our God never promised us that there wouldn't be storms in our lives, but rather that He would be beside us through those storms. He is with us when we are in the valleys and when we are on the mountaintops. For those who have a belief in the Lord there is hope, and a knowing that we will have eternal life if we have accepted Him into our hearts as our Lord and Savior.

During the time since J.T. and I began speaking in churches and then starting our ministry, I have been speaking about how I was able to get through the loss of my first husband. I have shared about J.T.'s battle with depression and suicidal ideation. I have talked about his suicide attempts and how I managed through it all. I have shared how I stayed beside JT., praying over him, loving him, knowing that God would heal him in His perfect timing. I have spoken about these and several other losses and tribulations that I have experienced that could have served to destroy my life.

My faith in God has sustained me through it all. I figured everyone has had to deal with all the same types of losses as me. Everyone has carried the same burdens I have. I knew that I was not alone.

Over the last couple of years, as I have shared my testimonies and shared what the Lord has placed on my heart, I've learned that people are shocked to hear all that I've been through. And they have been encouraged to hear about the strength of my faith in God through it all. That is not to minimize the trials others have carried. In fact, I know my experiences have not been as difficult as some others. It's how we choose to overcome. My faith has helped me to overcome circumstances that I simply could not have on my own.

The first time I spoke was at House of Purpose. It was a F.I.R.E. Friday event, just like my husband's experience the year before. I was scheduled to speak just 48 hours after having been anesthetized and undergoing a surgical procedure. The turnout was fantastic! The love my House of Purpose family showed me was beyond compare. They are genuine in their outpouring. I was blessed and humbled to have been asked to speak on that night.

As I speak and share my heart and my testimonies, my prayer is always the same. I pray that I can impact just that one who needs to hear what God can do for us if we are willing to surrender ourselves to Him. I pray that the message I share is something that God uses to transform someone's life, to draw someone closer to God. I always want to encourage others to lean not unto their own understanding, but to press into God.

Speaking at Pastor Dan Whitlock's church, I had the opportunity to touch the hearts of many. This was followed by a one-to-one meeting with a woman. She was seeking guidance about a burden she was carrying. It was a blessing to know that I could impact another person's life in this way.

On June 2nd, 2018, J.T. and I were invited to speak at men's and women's fellowship meetings, respectively. When I finished speaking that morning, I was greeted with so many warm hugs and words of encouragement. The women in attendance were encouraging me to continue sharing my story. Several told me that as I spoke they were thinking, *This woman has been through so much. It is in an incredible faith that she carries.* They desired to spend more time talking with me and have me minister to them. God allows us to use our pain, our experiences, to minister to others in their time of need.

Each time I have had the opportunity to speak, I have come away so full, so blessed, and so humbled as to how God has used me. It has been powerful to witness how my message resonates with so many people. Unless you have been in a church that is Spirit-filled, you just cannot imagine how much love and energy you can experience. It is absolutely overwhelming!

I continue to be amazed at how God is using my testimony to help others. I honestly never imagined I would be used in such a mighty way. For the longest time, I simply figured that I would share this with friends on a one-to-one basis. That I might speak with a friend to help them through a storm. I had no idea!

As I close this chapter, I want to acknowledge and thank the church leaders who have invited me to speak. I look forward to the work that God has ahead for me. I will continue to speak about the goodness of God and all that He has done for me.

I will continue to rebuke the enemy on a regular basis. As we draw closer to God, Satan comes at us harder. As we work in God's kingdom, as we engage in kingdom building, Satan will be on the attack. But, God. But, God will be there to bring us through every storm. He will be there to calm our minds, our spirits, our hearts.

If you haven't accepted Jesus as your Lord and Savior and want to experience the peace and love that envelops you always, I would encourage you to search your own heart. Ask, "Is Jesus in my heart? Is He my Lord and Savior?" If you take this step, you will be comforted. You will know that He is with you and He brings a peace that you may never have experienced before.

"And Ruth said, Intreat me not to leave thee, or to return from following after thee: for whither thou goest, I will go; and where thou lodgest, I will lodge: thy people shall be my people, and thy God my God."
Ruth 1:16 (KJV)

CHAPTER 17

CAN YOU MINISTER
OUR WEDDING?

Song of Solomon 4:10 (KJV)

"How fair is thy love, my sister, my spouse!
How much better is thy love than wine! And the smell of thine
ointments than all spices!"

As our work in ministry began, one of my younger brothers, Norman, asked if I would be able to officiate his eldest son's wedding. Bobby's eldest granddaughter, Taryn, asked me a similar question. She wanted to know if I would be able to perform her marriage when that day arrived. I was still trying to wrap my mind around all of this. I seemed to have to routinely remind myself that I was now formally involved in ministry. Once I received my ordination through House of Purpose, the doors were open for me to perform weddings. And so, it began.

Even before I officiated my first wedding, I was asked to conduct a vow renewal ceremony. This service was for a dear couple whom I met through this journey. They had traveled to hear me speak several times. They were celebrating their 30th wedding anniversary by renewing their wedding vows. Since no marriage license was involved, I consented to their request. It was a beautiful winter day in December. A small gathering of family and friends came together to witness and celebrate the occasion. At the conclusion of the vow renewal service, the couple invited me to share my testimony with those in attendance.

The first wedding I was asked to perform involved Norman's son, Ryan and his fiancée, Candace. My wife and I took the opportunity to sit down with them and discuss their faith. We talked about what they wanted in a wedding ceremony. We drafted a wedding program and shared it with them. Their wedding was scheduled for Friday, May 11th, 2018. It was to be an outdoor wedding at a country club near the hometown where I grew up.

A few weeks prior to the wedding date, I told my brother that I was looking forward to seeing them all on May 11th. He replied, "Don't you mean May 10th?" I smiled and nodded, and we parted company. As my wife and I made our way home that evening, I reflected on what my brother had said, "May 10th?" Oh my! I failed to account for the wedding rehearsal. I needed to be there for that. The problem was we lived more than three hours away from the venue and I had a conflict with my work schedule. How could I not be there to practice the evening before ministering my first wedding? We concocted a plan to have my wife travel to the venue earlier than me. She would stand in for me at the rehearsal. Then I would then be there on Friday evening for the real thing. It wasn't ideal, but I didn't know what else to do.

Three days prior to the rehearsal, I got a break. I learned that I was not a candidate to be interviewed for a job I once held. This development allowed me a little more flexibility when it came to my work schedule for the day of the rehearsal. I could travel to the venue with my wife. Thankfully, I could participate in the wedding rehearsal.

The wedding day arrived. I was a little nervous, but I felt good about how the rehearsal had gone the night before. The time came to assemble at the entrance to the outdoor venue. It was a sunny, warm day. The outdoor area only afforded shade around the perimeter. Those seated in the available chairs were in direct sunlight. Jokingly, a couple of folks cautioned me to not get too long-winded in my delivery. The groom and I made our entrance and took our place at the edge of the gazebo. I had a high-top table positioned just to my right to hold a bottle of water and my microphone. As I stood there watching the bridal party enter, I noticed that the microphone was not on the table. What now? *I guess I am just going to have to use my voice, unaided,* I thought.

Chapter 17: *Can You Minister Our Wedding?*

The service began, and it came time for me to speak I asked, "Who gives this woman to be married to this man?" The bride's father replied, "Her mother and I." He placed his daughter's hand in the hand of the groom and turned to go back to his seat. I continued with the service, which went very well. I was feeling pretty good about things. I even felt that I projected my voice well enough for everyone to hear, absent the microphone. When it was over, I approached Norman and asked him how it went. He put his hand on my shoulder and said, "That was powerful. You did a good job. I only have one suggestion for you. Next time, you might want to instruct everyone, 'That they may be seated.'" Immediately, I realized my gaffe. After the bride's father returned to his seat, I was supposed to give that instruction. I never did. Every one of the guests stood for the entire ceremony.

A week later, I would have an opportunity to redeem myself. I had already been scheduled to minister my second wedding. I had met this couple, Jacob Underwood and Courtney Waterman, through the mother of the groom and the father of the bride. My wife and I met with the soon-to-be-married couple several times in advance of the service, so we could get to know one another. The very first time I met with them, the future husband asked me, "What led you to get involved in ministry." I retorted, "Are you sure you want to ask me that question?" You guessed it. They heard a telling of the first several chapters of this book. Each time we would meet, the two of them would share incredible situations that they had experienced. They would ask Terri Lee and me about the latest in our ministry work.

Their wedding was also to be an outdoor wedding. The weather did not appear as if it was going to cooperate. We had the wedding rehearsal on Friday evening. We practiced under a tent, which covered a patio area that would be used for the reception following the ceremony. We practiced three times and things went well each time.

The next day, the weather appeared threatening throughout the day. It cleared just enough for the bride and groom to call an audible and move the ceremony to the vineyard. I had the script ready to go. In big, bold letters, I included a reminder to myself, "Inform the guests that they may be seated." As I made my way down to the vineyard, I discovered that only one bench was being provided for seating for the groom's parents and one bench for the bride's parents. I would not need to tell anyone that they may be seated, for the second service in a row.

We have a strong and growing prison ministry as I mentioned in an earlier chapter. I find it rather ironic that the grooms for the first two weddings I would minister are on the opposite end of the scales. The first groom is a corrections officer. The second groom is a police officer. What are the odds?

> *"Come, let us take our fill of love until the morning: let us solace ourselves with loves."*
> *Proverbs 7:18 (KJV)*

CHAPTER 18

MY WALK TO EMMAUS

2 Peter 2:21 (KJV)

"For it had been better for them not to have known the way of righteousness, than, after they have known it, to turn from the holy commandment delivered unto them."

Several times in the first couple of years following the accident and the beginning of this ministry, I have fought against a recurring lie. I have allowed doubts about the authenticity of this ministry into my mind. I have come to believe that the Devil did not like the work that God had begun through me. I had never been a factor in this spiritual realm before. At best, I was a fixture on the sideline, but more truly stated, I probably never even made it out of the locker room. As you will read in this chapter, I faced another attack about the authentic nature of this ministry.

On August 27th, 2015, just six days after the accident, I met a man at the funeral home visitation for my brother and sister-in-law. I was at the funeral home standing in the receiving line with the rest of my family. My brother and sister-in-law's flag-draped coffin was at the beginning of the line. Members of a fire department honor guard stood watch over the casket as a tribute to Bobby and Pam. Individuals from this unit would ceremoniously exchange places with each other as part of an established routine. Meanwhile, an estimated 1,200 – 1,500 people filed through to pay their respects and to console our grieving family.

I stood toward the end of the receiving line alongside my two brothers. With a spirit of reverence, but with a comfort of knowing where my brother and his wife were on this evening, I greeted those who passed through with an upbeat spirit. Dave Schuller was one of the many people who came through the line.

When Dave reached me, he came to a stop. He reached into his pocket and withdrew a piece of paper and handed it to me. He explained, this was your brother's completed Emmaus Walk application. He said, "Your brother turned it into me the night of the accident. He was planning to participate on the walk this fall."

I had only recently heard of the Emmaus Walk. An emergency management colleague and dear friend, Bob Suddarth, had informed me of one that existed in an area of Virginia known as the New River Valley. He had invited me to go, indicating that he would sponsor me. I politely told him I wasn't available. While it may have been true that I wasn't available to go on the spring or fall walks in 2014, the truth of the matter is that I wasn't in a place where I was interested in going. I wasn't living my life that way at the time.

The Walk to Emmaus seeks to create spaces in which participants can re-experience God's love and continue to grow in His grace. The Walk to Emmaus provides spaces for spiritual formation to occur. Emmaus communities exist in several areas within Virginia and other states and countries as well.

So, when Dave handed me my brother's completed application, two thoughts came to mind. *First, that's cool. I have something that my brother handled only six days ago. And secondly, why did Dave select me (out of all my family members present) to give it to?*

Dave was affiliated with the Emmaus Walk group based in Danville, Virginia, known as the Dan River Emmaus Community. For the 2016 and 2017 spring and fall walks, Dave would ask me if I was interested. Now, my life was being transformed in a major way, but I simply did not have the time to go when the walks were scheduled. At least, I was not willing to make it a great enough priority to go in 2016 and 2017.

As the 2018 spring walk approached, Dave asked again. "Would you be available to go this time?" I talked it over with my wife and agreed to have Dave sign me up. He asked for some information necessary for the application and submitted it on my behalf. I was all set. Dave would be my sponsor. The man who had received my brother's application; the man who had handed me this same completed application six days after receiving it from my brother; was now my sponsor for my walk.

The spring walk in 2018 was scheduled for April 12th – 15th. About ten days before I was to go on this experience, I was getting a sense that I needed to back out of it. I was beginning to regret the idea of allowing myself to be sponsored. I asked Dave what the repercussions were of not going. I had talked to my supervisor about the opportunities for additional work assignments that would prevent me from going. Dave spoke straight to me. He said, "There is a lot of effort that has gone into your participation in this experience. Only 36 people were selected to participate, and you were one of them. You need to go." Dave was speaking accountability into my life. I knew he was right. But I just did not want to go.

Right up until the day that we were to depart, I was looking for a reason that would justify me not going. I finally realized that I would be going. I then turned my focus differently. I was going to go on this Emmaus Walk, but I was going to use this experience to "quit God." I was going to go through the experiences of the next 72 hours. I was going to hear the messages that would be taught. I would participate in the exercises and activities, but only to a minimal level. Once Monday arrived, I would be able to set aside this ministry work and return to the life that I had once known. This didn't mean that I didn't believe in God anymore. It didn't mean that I would quit going to church, etc. I would just set aside the ministry work that had taken root in my life. I considered the idea of "quitting God" while experiencing this Emmaus Walk as being analogous to quitting smoking while touring a cigarette factory.

On the night we arrived, we received an orientation and an overview of what the schedule would look like over the next three days. We were encouraged to not overthink anything. We were encouraged to not anticipate what was to come. We were encouraged to just be in the moment. We were told that as we left the orientation we would walk to the chapel. We were instructed to maintain silence from the time we left orientation until we returned to the chapel the next morning. Don't try to get to know the others in your cabin. Just remain in silence and focus on your relationship with Jesus Christ and what you want to get out of this experience. I couldn't have been happier. The first night would be out of the way and I wouldn't have to speak to anyone. The other two men assigned to my cabin honored this request for silence. We didn't speak a word.

As I turned in for the night, I picked up one of the composition notebooks that I had brought with me. I had thought that I would write about my experiences over these days. I thought that my writing would cover my pre-arrival thoughts and attitudes and continue right through until arriving home on Sunday evening. That first night was the only time I wrote in the composition book. The last thing that I wrote was, "I came here to quit God."

I set the book down on a spare bunk, wrestled down into the bed, and pulled the blanket up over my shoulder. As I settled in the dark quietness of the evening, I heard in my spirit, "Be obedient and fast for three days." My first thought was, *Do what?* I have never fasted longer than 24 hours. I began to think of my fasting routine the few times I had fasted over the past two years. I recalled dear friends who had fasted for five days in sacrifice for a family to whom my wife and I had been ministering. So, I knew two people who had recently fasted longer than three days. My fasting routine had been conducted without others knowing. That would likely not be possible in this instance. Also, I had prepared myself for previous fasts. I would eat well in the time leading up to my fast. This had not happened in this instance, as I was not in the best of spirits coming into Emmaus and had not finished all of my dinner before arriving at the conference center. Lastly, I had never fasted from a perspective of obedience. It was always out of sacrifice in the past.

As I fell asleep on this first night, I did not know what I was going to do. It is awfully tough to quit God and be obedient to Him at the same time. What a conundrum.

When I awoke on Friday morning, things were still not clear to me. Was I really going to fast for the entirety of this experience? How will my lack of food affect my ability to participate? After leaving the chapel that morning, we headed to the cafeteria. The period of silence had been lifted and the conversations were flowing.

At this Emmaus Walk experience, the meals are served family style. Individuals were assigned one of eight seats at a table. Each meal, everyone is assigned to eat with different people. Both participants and team leadership are assigned to each table. The food is prepared and served by a team of volunteers. They want to make sure that each person has plenty of food, is served well, and their dietary needs are being met. Even up until this moment, I was not sure if I was going to fast.

Then, it happened. The first platter of food was served at the table where I was assigned. I saw this overflowing platter of bacon and biscuits making its way down my side of the table. As this platter was passed to me, it was as if I could not grab it. The platter passed right through my hands to the person sitting at the end of the table. *I guess this is it*, I thought. *I am really going to fast for the next three days.*

Immediately, those seated at my table noticed that I was not taking any of the, what I could only assume to be, delicious, breakfast items from the platters being passed around. And the questions began. "Are you not hungry? Do you not feel well? Do you not eat breakfast?" I did my best to deflect this first battery of questions, which were followed by questions from the volunteers who had prepared the food and were serving it. "Do you have special dietary restrictions? Is there something else we can get you? We can make you just about anything. What can we bring you?" Everyone was startled to hear that everything was alright and that I only wanted a glass of water.

As it turns out, it was not only the family-style meals that I had to endure, but there was an incredible spread laid out for break time between each meal. These spreads included assorted sodas, tea, and water. Bite-sized meats and cheeses were also offered along with vegetable platters, crackers and a selection of items to satisfy each person's sweet tooth. And, to boot, bowls of candies, gum, and mints were placed at each table when the biblical messages and talks were being delivered.

Lunch time on Friday arrived. Again, we filed into the cafeteria. We located our assigned seat which rotated to a different location with each meal. For this meal, I was situated between two of the weekend's team leaders. In fact, the man to my left was the Laity Leader, Steve Smith, for the weekend. The man to my right was one of the assistant table leaders. Being in the company of a whole new group of men led to another barrage of questions about the fact that I was not eating. The Laity Leader asked me a couple of questions himself. Finally, he asked me, "Are you fasting?" I explained that I was. He stated, almost in disbelief, "I have never heard of anyone coming on an Emmaus Walk and fasting."

The man sitting to my right, Barry Arnold, began to ask me some questions about my faith journey. As our conversation unfolded, he quickly put two and two together. He asked me, "Are you Bobby Clark's brother?" When I told him that I was, he explained that he led the Kairos Prison Ministry team out of Floyd County. He said that the Tuesday before the accident that claimed Bobby's life, Bobby had attended an informational/orientation session concerning joining the Kairos Prison Ministry team. He was intrigued about the development of our ministry and the work that we had begun in terms of prison ministry.

As Friday ended, I had avoided eating anything all day. I had consumed water, but no food, snacks, candies, or other beverages. I went to bed for the evening.

As Saturday began, I made it through breakfast, the morning snack, and lunch. As the day progressed, I was experiencing greater levels of angst. I reflected on the fact that my brother had a desire to complete this Emmaus Walk. My brother had a desire to serve in ministry. He lived this life. He pursued this life. This was not on my radar at all. While my brother pursued it; it just fell on me. I questioned if I truly heard that I was to fast. I questioned the validity of the ministry that my wife and I had established. I questioned my authenticity in all of this. I wondered if I was living as a poser in ministry. *Was I an imposter?* When break times occurred, I found opportunities to spend time reading scripture and taking short walks. I considered walking out the front gate of the conference center and finding my own way home. I really wanted to escape.

Sometime during the late afternoon on Saturday, there was a group activity planned that would be celebratory in nature. I had reached a point that I simply did not want to participate in this specific activity. I approached the member of the leadership team who was my assigned table leader for the weekend. I asked him if I could sit this activity out. I told him that there wasn't anything specific about this activity to which I was reacting, I just did not want to participate. I apologized for seeking a variance to the protocol and rules for the weekend activities. I simply wanted to sit outside of this building on the curb to reflect and gather my thoughts.

To my surprise, my table leader told me he did not think that would be a problem, but that he wanted to check with the other leadership. A few minutes later a man named Keith emerged. Keith seemed to be responsible for much of the weekend logistics. He told me he was going to grab a golf cart and he and I would just ride around the conference center grounds. As I climbed onto the cart, Keith told me that he wasn't going to try to get me to talk. He said, "I am not even going to say that much to you. I just want to be sure you are okay."

We rode around the compound and Keith shared a little bit of his testimony with me. We arrived at an area on a hillside above a pond and he brought the cart to a stop. We just sat there in the peaceful quiet of an early summer evening. As we sat there, I began to tell Keith about first meeting Dave. I told him about how Dave gave me my brother's completed Emmaus Walk application. As I was beginning to speak to Keith, the spiritual leader for the weekend popped over the hill and sat on the bank above the pond.

The spiritual leader (or lead pastor) for this particular walk was a man named Seth Robertson of Compassion Church – Axton. When he sat down, he made similar remarks to me as Keith had. "I am not here to get you to talk. I am not going to say a whole lot to you. I don't know much of your story. I just want to be sure you are alright."

After a few minutes passed, I climbed out of the golf cart and walked over to the bank where Seth was sitting and plopped down beside him. Keith also exited the cart and walked back to the conference area. As I sat next to Seth, I began to give him the scope of that with which I was wrestling — from meeting Dave at the funeral home; to knowing my brother had a desire to complete this experience; to never feeling though I had grieved their passing; to feeling like a ministry imposter. I shared the testimony of the accident and going to court on behalf of C.J. Martin. I then talked about the ministry outreach in which my wife and I were involved. Suddenly another man appeared. It was pastor Gary Robertson, Seth's father.

When Seth was headed to the location where Keith had brought me, Seth passed by his father, who was preparing his talk for Sunday. Seth told his dad, "I am not sure what I am going to run into, but I may need your help." Gary joined his son at the bank above the pond.

As Gary approached, I was concluding with the nature of our ministry outreach. I had shared that we had been assisting a homeless family, including having them move into our basement for a brief period. I had explained that we had prepared to move in a man who had been released from a regional jail and was trying to get himself re-established. Gary and

Seth spoke of a program offered through their church known as the Hope Center. They offered that we should consider some opportunities for our ministries to collaborate. If I knew of candidates that would benefit from their program, we could work together to enroll these individuals in the Hope Center for twelve months.

Through our time together, my spirits were lifted. The work that my wife and I were engaged in was legitimized. I received confirmation that I was authentic. God used these men to speak truth into my life. Seth went on to say, "I need to find an opportunity to have you come and speak at our church."

It was time to rejoin the others for the balance of the evening activities. I felt relieved. I went to God in prayer. I asked him, "Is the fast lifted?" The response I heard was, "Be patient. Sunday's coming."

The Laity Leader approached me a brief time later. He said, "I know you are fasting, and I hate to tell you this, but we are having an ice cream social this evening. I know you won't eat any ice cream, but I need you to go into the cafeteria with everyone else. He encouraged me to express appreciation to the volunteers who had traveled there to serve the ice cream. I explained that it was no problem. I would cooperate.

As I entered the cafeteria, another member of the leadership team, who I had not spoken with during my time at the program, approached me. He said, "Before you go to bed this evening, I need to talk with you." His name is Ken. I wasn't sure what he wanted, but he said it with enough intensity that I knew there was something that he had to say. I watched for Ken to finish his ice cream and since I was not eating any, I approached him when I saw that his bowl was empty. I asked him if he was ready to talk. He suggested we step outside.

Once we were outside, Ken told me, "I have been trying to figure it out for a couple of days. I know who you are." I must have had a puzzled look on my face. He went on to say, "Let me tell you who I am." He said, "I am a volunteer firefighter with the Bassett Volunteer Fire Department. I was on the scene of the ambulance fire that night back in August 2015. In fact, I was one of the first people to arrive at the scene of your brother's accident. I was there trying to console Mr. Martin and his son." He went on to explain, "Not only am I a volunteer firefighter, I am also our department's chaplain."

Ken said as he stood there trying to comfort and console Mr. Martin and his son, the group of bikers arrived on the scene. He said, "There I was, and this gang of bikers arrived at the scene." I spoke to God and said, "I don't know who you thought you were sending, but I am not cut out for this. Of course, we had no idea who they were." He said as he approached the group in an effort to keep them away from the driver of the truck and the emergency responders, the leader explained that his rules did not apply in this situation and they made their way to Mr. Martin.

Ken explained that as part of the leadership team, they are discouraged from bringing any type of logo apparel with them for the weekend. He said, "As I was packing, I placed a certain t-shirt in my bag." I thought, "What am I doing? I cannot take that with me." And I removed the t-shirt and set it down alongside my bag. He said, "As I continued to finish packing, something was nagging at me to bring the t-shirt. I put it back in my bag. I wasn't sure why I did this until just now." Ken reached in his back pocket and handed me a folded-up Bassett Volunteer Fire Department t-shirt and said, "This is for you."

I asked Ken if he had been present on May 1st, 2017 when I was invited to speak to the membership of the Bassett Volunteer Fire Department. He explained that he had not been there. He told me that he was afraid that it would be too difficult to hear what I had to say. I told him there were a few details he needed to understand. And so, we continued talking into the evening.

As I returned to my assigned cabin, one of the men also assigned to my cabin said, "There is something I have to tell you. I wasn't sure if I was going to tell you, but I realize that I have to tell you this." He informed me that he worked for the Virginia Department of Transportation out of the Axton, VA office. He said, "One of my coworkers is a man named Billy Byrd." I don't know Billy Byrd, but my jaw dropped, and I knew exactly what he was going to tell me. He said, "Billy is Dickie Byrd's brother." Dickie Byrd was the Virginia State Trooper who investigated my brother's accident. The man telling me this, D.J., explained that he lived a few houses away from the trooper. He talked about the impact this entire situation had on him as a trooper.

I told D.J. to let Trooper Byrd, who has since retired from the Virginia State Police, know how much our family appreciated what he did for us. I told D.J. to tell him that he was my hero and that I loved him.

By the time I laid down to sleep on Saturday night, my head was just spinning. So much had happened through the weekend. I realized that my efforts to "quit God" had failed.

Arriving in the cafeteria on Sunday morning, I continued what had become my routine. I skipped all of the incredible food and drank a glass of water.

After two more talks on Sunday morning, it was now time for lunch. We were told that this would be the final meal of the weekend. We were informed that a special experience awaited us in the cafeteria. We were encouraged to remain silent as we left the meeting room to line up outside the cafeteria.

While filing out of the meeting room, one of the men assigned to the same small group as me, approached. He said, "I understand you know something about forgiveness." This individual and I had not spoken much to each other all weekend. Frankly, that was true of most of the people with whom I was participating. I was trying to lay low and not connect with others. Remember, I was trying, albeit unsuccessfully, to quit God. When he made this comment to me, I proceeded to tell him just a couple of sentences about my story.

Quickly, the conversation shifted to him telling me about a situation in which he had struggled in the area of receiving forgiveness. As we entered the cafeteria, we were standing in close proximity to one another and I was listening intently as he whispered his story to me. Suddenly, we embraced. I later explained to my wife that I had not been hugged that hard, that tightly, and for that long since I was in the courtroom with C.J.

As we hugged one another, I began to pray over him. I spoke words of life, love, and healing over his life. A couple of folks from the leadership team approached us. I waved them off. As I finished the prayer, I heard clearly and audibly in my left ear, "Your fast was for him." My knees buckled. Had he not been holding me up, I would have collapsed on the floor.

For this meal, there were no assigned seats. Following the blessing, each person chose a seat and sat down. As I sat down, I said a prayer to God. "Am I allowed to eat this meal?" The response I heard was, "If you choose not to eat this meal, it isn't because of Me." I just remember how incredible the green beans that were served onto my plate tasted.

Following lunch, we returned to the meeting room for our next speaker. As the worship music began to play, two pastors, Seth and Scott, approached me. Quite directly, Seth stated, "J.T., we need to see you outside." I was surprised and uncertain as to what the reason for this could be. I wondered, "What have I done wrong now?"

When we arrived outside, Seth explained what was about to happen had never happened before that he was aware. He said, "Our pastoral team takes care of this." He went on to say, "But our next speaker is insisting that you come and pray over him before the next talk." I had no idea who the next speaker was or why I would be summoned to pray for him. As we walked from the meeting room to the prayer room where this man was located, I heard a final message, "I told you Sunday was coming." When we arrived at the prayer room, there was the next speaker, Dave Schuller. I assembled with the other pastors. We laid hands on Dave and prayed over him.

At the conclusion of the program, each participant was invited to say a few words about their experience. There were 36 of us to speak. We needed to limit our comments to 2-3 minutes. We were informed to state our name, what table or group we were assigned for the weekend, what was profound about our experience, and how we would apply it when we got back home.

When it was my turn, I stated, "My name is J.T. Clark. I am from the table, 'I am.' I came here this weekend to 'quit God.' When I settled in the first night, I was told, 'Be obedient and fast for three days.' Earlier today, I was moved to pray over a man who had asked me about forgiveness. As I finished praying over him, God revealed to me that my fast was for him. My fast was for a man that I had not even known at the time God asked me to be obedient and fast. What am I going to do when I go back to my home community? I am going to continue to 'Love God. And, Love People.'"

On the way home Sunday evening, Dave, who not only sponsored me, but also provided me transportation to and from the conference center, shared with me some of the observations made by some on the leadership team. He said that several times he was approached by leaders inquiring if I was okay. They wondered if they should intercede. Dave said, "I just kept telling them that you were going to be alright. Things would work themselves out. Just trust the process."

The Walk to Emmaus afforded me several opportunities as I continued maturing and growing in my faith. I was grieving Bobby and Pam's passing in a way that I had not yet done to that point. While the leadership expressed concerns with my well-being, they allowed me the space and provided the support I needed for things to process. The format of the weekend program is a group experience, but it is an individual process. Each participant is at a different stage in his faith walk. Each of us were working through different situations.

I had access to individuals identified as Table Leaders, Assistant Table Leaders, Lay Speakers, Spiritual Speakers, pastoral leadership, etc. At no time was I compelled to participate in any activity. We were routinely reminded that we would receive from the experience based upon what we invested in the process.

The weekend program afforded opportunities for individual fellowship, small-group activities, multiple chapel services, worship time, and prayer. The weekend also included fifteen talks, each building off the previous. While the speakers prepared and delivered their own messages, the themes for each talk served as a building block. I saw the way these talks dovetailed together as a powerful revelation through the Holy Spirit.

A final perspective about my fasting experience…I have lost 65 pounds over the past 2½ years. When I arrived home, I was curious about how much weight I had lost given that I had not eaten for the past couple of days. When I stepped onto the scale, there was no change in my weight from Thursday morning. I thought to myself, *That's curious.* As I stepped off the scale, I heard, "I told you the fast was for him. It wasn't for you."

The Holy Spirit moved in a mighty way during my Walk to Emmaus experience. Most notably was through the message I received that first night as I climbed into bed, "Be obedient and fast for three days." But, during another segment of the program I was given an opportunity to lay down a burden I was carrying. For me, the burden was a spirit of timidity. The Holy Spirit was calling for me to be bold in my faith. While others were laying down burdens that seemed much heavier and weightier, He moved me to step out and speak to my mountain.

The people who surrounded me on the Walk to Emmaus experience were there to teach, lead, worship, and encourage. Through their teaching, fellowship, and worshiping, I was provided an opportunity to grow in my faith, step deeper into my relationship with Jesus Christ, and was emboldened to embrace the calling God placed on my life.

On Monday, following my Walk to Emmaus, I received a text message from my Table Leader. He asked me how the day was going. I interpreted his text message to be a standard communication that each Table Leader sent to each participant assigned to their group. I sent a generic response that all was well. We engaged in a brief text exchange that led to a telephone call lasting more than two hours. During the call, this Table Leader revealed the impact my Walk to Emmaus had on him. He said, "I might have been the Table Leader by title, but truthfully, I was taking more from you. It was as if you were the Table Leader." He went on to explain a personal matter where he chose to move in forgiveness in a years-old situation following the closing ceremony on Sunday evening.

While I was resisting further advances in ministry work, God showed me in a powerful way that He has me on a course. I have been chosen to continue the work that my brother began. This lineage ministry is real, if I will only continue to surrender myself, humble myself, and be obedient to what He is calling me to do. The message I received that first night, "Be obedient and fast for three days," was a challenge to determine where I stood. God revealed the authenticity of this ministry through that experience. He revealed to me through others who were on this journey, that through obedience, lives are impacted. From the participant who revealed his pain to me; the Table Leader who shared how he was impacted by my story; the Laity Leader who witnessed how I managed through the weekend; to the Spiritual Leader who heard my testimony (and along with his father) and talked about how we could partner together and invited me to his church to speak less than two months later; God showed me the impact He could have through my ministry.

Things in our ministry have intensified since the time of my Walk to Emmaus. I have been invited to lead a ministry hour at the county jail on Wednesday mornings. The speaking opportunities have continued to come. Those who have heard me speak and preach pre- and post-Emmaus have noticed a boldness that did not exist before. While I was not selected as a member of the team for the next Walk to Emmaus experience, I intend to serve behind the scenes to support others who are embarking on the same journey that I experienced.

"And if it seem evil unto you to serve the LORD, choose you this day whom ye will serve; whether the gods which your fathers served that were on the other side of the flood, or the gods of the Amorites, in whose land ye dwell: but as for me and my house, we will serve the LORD."
Joshua 24:15 (KJV)

CHAPTER 19

A FAMILY CIRCLE

1 John 4:7 (KJV)

"Beloved, let us love one another; for love is of God; and every one that loveth is born of God, and knoweth God."

This final story I want to include involves a family who has turned up in our lives over and over since the one-year anniversary of the accident. They have surfaced in so many ways, so many times, it was difficult to know where to place them in the chronology of the overall story. So, I have included it here. The first encounter was one led by the Holy Spirit, a God-moment I will call it.

On August 15th, 2016, I was having dinner at a local restaurant in Rocky Mount, VA called Ippy's Restaurant. My wife had not been feeling well that evening and she encouraged me to go out and get myself some dinner. I sat alone in the main dining area, eating and reflecting on the events that would take place in the weekend ahead, commemorating the one-year anniversary.

As I sat at my table alone, a large group of people, seemingly from one family, entered the dining room. They were seated at a large, round table in the center of the room, but shaded toward my end. I could not help but witness the festive nature of their evening. They were certainly enjoying one another's company. I believe there were eleven people in their party. At that point, I did not know them. I did not interact with them during the course of the dinner except to acknowledge that they were having a wonderful family time together.

As I was finishing my dinner, I heard a message in my spirit, "Pay for their meal." I had grown accustomed to receiving such messages to move in the lives of other people, but this seemed a bit extreme. There were eleven people having a full dinner celebrating some occasion. I texted my wife. I told her that I believed that I was being led by the Holy Spirit to pick up the dinner tab for a large table of people. I asked her what I should do about it. Without hesitation or question, my wife responded, "If you believe you have heard from the Holy Spirit, you had better be obedient." My wife had decided over the past year that we would use the difference between what the fine was and what it could have been to bless the lives of people who came across our paths. We would follow the lead of the Holy Spirit in such circumstances.

It wasn't often that I did this, but in this situation, I wrote a note that would be delivered to their table after I left. A few days later, this anonymous note would surface on Facebook. The note read:

"FAMILY TIME!! Nothing like it.

You are being blessed tonight. The cost of your dinner and tip have been paid. You might wonder why.

My brother and sister-in-law were killed in a motorcycle accident just about one year ago. Our family moved on a path of forgiveness toward the driver involved. We understood it was an accident.

When the driver of the truck had to go to court, I was moved by the Holy Spirit to go on his behalf. I was instructed by the Holy Spirit to pay his fine.

When the judge heard what I was there to do, he reduced the charge and fined the man $5.00. What could have been a fine of thousands of dollars was only $5.00.

My wife and I have decided to use the difference between what the fine could have been as compared to what it was to bless other people. You were chosen for this blessing tonight. Wrap one another in love. Know that God loves you. And enjoy your time together.

I handed this note to the manager with the instruction to deliver it after I left. I never anticipated I would hear anything else about it.

A couple of days passed, and I received a text message from a man named Wayne Scott. Wayne had worked with me at Carilion Franklin Memorial Hospital from 2007 – 2013. Wayne's text message simply said, "I know what you did." I asked him what he was talking about. He proceeded to tell me through text messages that his next-door neighbors (Freda and Sonny Nichols) had shared with him this incredible surprise that had happened during Freda's birthday celebration at Ippy's Restaurant. I thought to myself, that was supposed to be anonymous. I never signed the note and didn't want them to know.

The next month, our eldest daughter, Jordan, was getting married. She was marrying a man named Michael Nallen. Their wedding date was scheduled for Saturday, September 24th. Jordan had arranged to have her wedding cake and cupcakes made and delivered by a local bakery known as the Kupkakery Bakery located in Rocky Mount. She had already delivered a deposit for the order. On Friday, September 16th, I visited the bakery with the intent of paying off the balance.

When I arrived at the bakery, a young lady named Ashley Smith Boyd was working. I told her why I was there, and she explained that I would have to speak with the owner, Desiree Smith. The owner was away from the shop, but Ashley expected her back in about 20 minutes. I told her no problem. I would be more than happy to wait. As Ashley went about her work, I could sense that she wasn't having the best of days, I spoke to her and shared some encouraging words. She said, "There is something different about you." I explained that I had not always been this way. I asked her if she would like to hear a story while she worked. She said she would. I began to tell her about the accident and the court case.

As I got about 2/3 of the way through the story, Desiree Smith entered the bakery. She listened intently as I finished the story. When I got to the end, Ashley introduced me to Desiree. Desiree asked, "I just heard the end of the story. Would you mind starting at the beginning so that I can hear it all?" I consented and proceeded to tell it again. At about 2/3 of the way through the story, four customers entered the store. They listened to the last part. When I finished, this group asked if I would start at the beginning. I ended up sharing this testimony three times that Friday afternoon. Ashley and Desiree told me they are familiar with T.R.A.S.H. Ministry. They explained that their uncle attends services there. His name is Wayne Smith. His wife is Cindy. I knew Wayne well. He and Cindy had moved in my life deeply since the accident.

Following this, the owner, Desiree Smith, asked me, "You didn't come in here just to tell us this story. What did you come in here for?" I explained,

"I think I was here to share evidence of God's grace, love, and mercy." I also said that I had come there to make the final payment on the order for the Clark/Nallen wedding. She asked, "Are you Jordan's father? She is the sweetest young lady." She said, "Let me find the paperwork for her order." She disappeared into the back of the bakery. After a few minutes she reappeared. She said, "I cannot take any money from you. I am considering your account 'paid in full.' You don't owe anything." I was humbled by the gesture and shared the news with my wife, Jordan and Michael, and my House of Purpose family.

On the day of the wedding, the catering firm *Center Stage Catering* arrived at the venue. I worked with them to get set up for the reception. One woman who was working as a member of the catering team spoke with me. Her name is Teresa Blankenship. She told me that she knew who I was and what I had done. She told me that she was at the dinner at Ippy's Restaurant the month before when I paid for the birthday dinner for Freda Nichols. Freda is her sister-in-law. She talked about how moved everyone was to have received such a gift. She also said that she was related to Desiree Smith at the Kupkakery. I was having difficulty processing it all.

In October, Freda Nichols and I had the opportunity to speak. She wanted to do something to express her appreciation for what I had done for her birthday dinner. She also shared with me that her father-in-law, Bud Nichols, who is also a pastor, was having health issues and was in need of prayer. She told me that Pastor Bud was at the dinner at Ippy's Restaurant as well that night. He was moved by my act of obedience to the Holy Spirit. Freda shared that he was hospitalized and asked if I would visit him at the hospital and pray for healing over him. I assured her I would. And I did. Pastor Bud recovered. He and I have had several encounters since that first night at Ippy's Restaurant.

Freda and her husband, Sonny, have a small business. They host paint night events. Participants pay a few dollars to paint a picture that is selected especially for that particular event. Freda leads the participants, instructing them how to paint. Amongst other talents, Freda is an art teacher at the Benjamin Franklin Middle School in Franklin County, VA.

As the holidays were approaching, I had an idea. I asked Freda if we could arrange a private paint night. I wanted to set this event up as a Christmas present for my wife. I wanted to arrange it for a night that our three daughters would be home. Freda agreed to work with me. We talked about a venue and agreed that it would be fitting to use the private party room at Ippy's Restaurant. Freda and Sonny would not accept any money for their time and instruction. We scheduled the event for the Tuesday night before Thanksgiving 2016. It would be a surprise.

I arranged with our middle daughter, Caitlin, to take her mother out for the afternoon and then bring her to Ippy's for dinner. I had invited Terri Lee's closest friends and some other women who were connected to our story in some way. They assembled at the restaurant and we arranged for some heavy appetizers to be enjoyed by those in attendance. With everyone in place, Caitlin delivered her mother right on time. Mission accomplished! We pulled off the surprise. She could not have expected to receive a Christmas present like that two days before Thanksgiving. While the women enjoyed the paint night, Pastor Mike Price and I had dinner in the main dining room at the restaurant. Mike's wife, Stephanie, was a part of the paint night experience.

At this paint night event, an idea was hatched. Terri Lee's best friend, Dawn Rorrer, wanted to raise money to help a self-employed farrier who had been injured months earlier in a terrible accident involving a horse. Randy Tuck's leg had been badly injured and required multiple surgeries and a long road to recovery. Dawn wanted to work with Freda and Sonny to host paint nights across Franklin and Floyd counties with the proceeds going to benefit Randy. These benefit paint night events took root.

Fast forward to the Walk to Emmaus. You may remember, the Laity Director for the walk was a man named Steve Smith. There were two Steve Smiths that were part of the leadership team for this walk. We called them Steve Smith Virginia and Steve Smith North Carolina. Steve Smith Virginia was the Laity Director. As it turns out, he is also the cousin of Sonny Nichols. Sonny is the husband of Freda Nichols. These two were at the original birthday dinner at Ippy's Restaurant.

Steve shared with me that he knew about what I had done at the dinner. Steve's wife, Becky, was part of the behind-the-scenes team that volunteered at this particular Walk to Emmaus. I was able to meet her as well. Steve Smith and Wayne Smith are brothers. Wayne was also on the same Walk event as me. Our relationship deepened during this experience.

On Saturday evening of the Walk, Steve Smith Virginia informed me that there was an ice cream social for all to enjoy. He acknowledged that I was fasting but informed me that I needed to be in the dining hall for the social regardless. I understood and attended. Steve pointed out to me that there were two more volunteers who had traveled to be a part of the ice cream social. Freda and Sonny Nichols were on hand that evening to serve ice cream to the leadership and participants.

Now back to paint night, on Saturday, April 21st, 2018, Terri Lee and I attended a benefit paint night organized by Dawn for the benefit of Randy. Freda and Sonny were leading and instructing this paint night. This was just six days after coming off my Walk to Emmaus. I had the opportunity to speak with Sonny about my experience and my plan to "quit God." I told him that I had been challenged on several occasions during the past couple of years with a sense that our ministry was just not real.

Then Sonny shared a revelation with me. He said, "You don't know do you? You don't get it, do you?" I wasn't certain what he meant. He said, "You don't understand your connection to these benefit paint nights that we have been conducting these past couple of years." I confessed that I did not know what he meant. Sonny proceeded to tell me their business plan for their paint night business was transformed. He said that he and Freda decided on an alternate pathway after my act of obedience in paying for the birthday dinner twenty months earlier. That act of obedience had compelled them to want to do something to give back to others in need. When Dawn approached them with the idea of doing a paint night to benefit Randy, they knew what they needed to do. I was floored! I could hardly believe what I was hearing. Tears welled up in my eyes and a warm, spirit-filled feeling surged through my body. I did not have the foggiest idea that one had to do with the other. Sonny said, "Your ministry is very authentic. You are impacting people all over through your words, your actions, your love, and your obedience."

The family circle continues. On the next day, Sunday, April 22nd, I was driving back from visiting my nephew at the Bland Correctional Center. I had stopped for a bite to eat. I had a Facebook Messenger exchange with a man named Paul Smith. Paul was also part of the leadership team at the Walk to Emmaus. I had received a Facebook friend request from a woman named Desiree Smith. The only woman named Desiree that I could remember meeting was the woman who owned the Kupkakery Bakery in Rocky Mount. When I looked at her Facebook profile, I saw that she was married to the Paul Smith who was the same guy on my Emmaus Walk.

In my Messenger exchange with Paul, I asked him if he had anything to do with the Kupkakery Bakery. He explained that his wife owned it. I asked him if he was familiar with the gesture his wife made concerning waiving the balance owed on my daughter's order for the wedding cake and desserts. He said that his wife had just shared the story of this occurrence from September 16th, 2016 at church that very morning on April 22nd, 2018. He went on to confirm with me that Wayne and Steve Smith Virginia were his uncles.

Now, for one final twist in all of this, Paul continued and informed me that he knew a man named Andy Bandy. He told me that it is his understanding that I also know Andy. Paul said that when he returned to work following the Walk to Emmaus experience, he shared with Andy and a couple of others about this guy he met during the walk that had an incredible testimony. Andy shared with Paul that he knew that guy and had heard the story before. Andy explained that I had invited Andy to sing at a special, mid-week service in support of a message that I would be preaching at House of Purpose. Andy told Paul that he had informed me that there was no way for him to get off work in time to get to House of Purpose for that service. Paul informed Andy that he would work something out. Andy accepted my offer to sing on May 9th, 2018 at the special service that I would be preaching. Paul not only did that, but then he showed up at House of Purpose to attend the service and be ministered through word and song.

The paths of the Clark, Nichols, and Smith families continue to intersect. Our combined story has not unfolded completely.

You cannot make this stuff up!

"The steps of a good man are ordered by the Lord: and He delighteth in his ways."
Psalm 37:23 (KJV)

CHAPTER 20

HERE IT IS...IN BLACK AND WHITE

1 Peter 4:8 (KJV)

"And above all things have fervent charity among yourselves: for charity shall cover the multitude of sins."

If you have made it to this chapter of the book, one of two things have happened. Either you are the type of person who likes to read the last chapter first. Or, you were compelled enough by the stories I have shared to want to know more. You may have arrived at this final chapter wondering, *So what? As a reader, what, if anything, does this have to do with my life?* To borrow a line from the title, let me give it to you plain and simple. Here it is spelled out in black and white.

This story is about many things. It is about forgiveness. It is about removing barriers for someone so that he is able to receive the forgiveness being offered. It is about love. It is about putting someone else and their needs ahead of your own. It is about hope. It is about demonstrating to those who were witnesses to different parts of this story, that we can choose differently. It is about unity. It is about stepping out and loving another person that is different from you. It is about not allowing race to impede our actions to love and forgive another. It is about grace. It is about stepping in to take a penalty that you do not owe. It is about mercy. It is about stepping in to thwart a penalty the world says is deserved. But for me, above all else, it is a story about obedience. It is about being obedient to the will of God. It is about moving to forgive another as it is written in the Bible. It is about moving to forgive as I received instruction in my spirit that day driving to court.

I was restless in the days leading up to C.J.'s court appearance. I knew I was being compelled to go. I just didn't want to go. I drove the opposite direction from the courthouse that morning to go to my place of employment. There came a moment when I simply needed to be obedient in making the trip to the courthouse. I rationalized that I needed to be in the courtroom for my brother. As I made the one-hour drive to the courthouse, it was then that I had the message come across my spirit, "I need you to pay the fine." I did not want to go to court. It was not my idea to pay the fine. It was not my idea to talk to the state trooper. I did not want to find myself standing in front of the judge. And it certainly was not my idea to say anything in the matter being heard that day. I found myself walking in obedience to what I was called to do.

In the months immediately following the court case and continuing, C.J. and I developed an incredible bond. We would talk frequently. On June 10th, 2016, I drove C.J. to visit Torrey at the New River Valley Regional Jail. It would be the first time that the two of them would meet. This meeting would take place through a video conferencing system. C.J. was a pastor so he could visit the facility on Fridays.

Following their visit, C.J. shared a little of their interaction with me. Think about that experience for just a moment. Consider the position in which C.J. found himself. Think about Torrey's situation. C.J. told me in a voice not much above a whisper, "Within the first three minutes of our visit, Torrey told me he forgave me." Yes. Both Torrey and Robin are their parents' children. It was overwhelming for C.J.

On our ride home from the jail, I asked C.J. a question. You must remember, I was very raw in terms of my spiritual growth. I asked C.J., "What would have happened if I had not been obedient to the instruction I received as I was driving to the courthouse?" His response was very humble, but it was also matter-of-fact. He said, "I am confident that my God was going to take care of me. You would have just missed out." That stunned me. Several months after this, I would later learn another detail. The people from T.R.A.S.H. Ministry had planned to give C.J. and Fernanda an amount of money that they would have spent on the fine. They were not in the courtroom that day, but they had planned to make them whole, financially speaking.

If you consider yourself a Christian, if you have a relationship with Jesus Christ, then the Holy Bible is the playbook for your life. In the aftermath of the accident, some said, "There just is no text book for how to deal with something of this magnitude." Oh, but there is. The Holy Bible lays it all out. A man named Johnell Manns, elder at House of Purpose shared his perspective of what makes a Christian. With his permission, I have included it here.

> *"Christians are good people getting better at being themselves. They are modest in their dress and seasoned in their speech; generous in their giving and bold in their testimony. Grateful in their blessings and generous in their giving; wise in their counsel, merciful in their scolding, serious about responsibility. When you are a professional, you back it up."*
> – *Elder Johnell Manns, House of Purpose*

Maybe you already made the decision to be a disciple of Jesus Christ before you ever heard of this book. Maybe you're on your faith walk and you're struggling in an area of your life. Maybe someone hurt you when you were little, and you have harbored anger and resentment toward that person or situation. Maybe the person who inflicted the pain is no longer even alive. Maybe you have an ongoing issue with a family member. Maybe you are angry at God. It's possible you have an issue with a co-worker or neighbor. As a disciple of Christ, as a Christian, we must move in forgiveness. The Bible tells us that if we don't forgive, we won't be forgiven. (See Matthew 6:15.)

Let's look at this in black and white. When it comes to the question of salvation there are no gray areas. You are either in or you are out. You have either accepted the gift of salvation, repented of your sin, and are growing in your faith, or you have not. You are either walking in forgiveness or you're holding onto an unforgiving heart. The Bible tells us that today is the day of salvation. (See 2 Corinthians 6:2.)

If you don't consider yourself a Christian, but this book has you thinking about it, I want to share a couple of points with you. First off, I do not advocate for a religion or a denomination. For me, it is all about a personal relationship with Jesus Christ. It's personal! Our heavenly Father sent His one and only Son to earth.

"For God so loved the world, that He gave His only begotten Son, that whosoever believeth in Him should not perish, but have everlasting life." John 3:16 (KJV)

He walked this planet as man. He lived a sinless life. In an act of obedience, Jesus Christ did the will of His Father and allowed Himself to be hung on a cross. He went to the cross to bear the penalty for our sins. He went to the cross to make a way for us to be united in heaven, through Him as our Lord and Savior, with our Heavenly Father. The Bible tells us,

"For all have sinned and come short of the glory of God." Romans 3:23 (KJV)

You must acknowledge Jesus Christ as your Lord and Savior. You must confess that you are a sinner and commit to a life of repentance. This is an act of turning away from the sinful life you previously lived. And, you must invite Jesus into your life, into your heart. There does not need to be a grand ceremony. In fact, you do not have to be in a church to do this. Many people do choose to answer an invitation to approach the altar during a church service. This is not a requirement. The altar of your heart is the most important place where you accept Christ. Stepping out during an invitation or altar call as part of a church service is an outward demonstration of your faith. I would never discourage that. But if your decision to follow Jesus Christ does not result in a heart-change, then you may need time to reflect on your intention, talk to another Christian, etc.

I had accepted Jesus as my Savior when I was a teenager, but I did not live a changed life. I struggled mightily as I tried to live my faith. For me, I was captive to not being able to move in forgiveness toward someone who had hurt me. I lived with a victim's mentality. I experienced a breakthrough in that way of thinking in February 2009. I finally moved in forgiveness toward that person who had hurt me. I was moved to demonstrate forgiveness in a number of circumstances between 2009 and 2015 when the accident occurred. This most recent act, in the case of my brother's accident, set me free, completely.

Don't expect to hear bells or have an emotional high when you decide to accept Jesus Christ as your Lord and Savior. However, you should begin to experience a change in the way you think about some things that you used to enjoy. I would highly encourage you to find a solid, Bible-believing and teaching church. Get your hands on a Bible and begin to get into His

Word. Learn of the promises that are in that book. Learn what is expected of you as a Christian.

The late, Reverend Billy Graham is credited with saying, "Salvation is free. Discipleship will cost you everything." As you study and devote your energies and interests to learning of the ways of Jesus, you will, or may, lose interest in worldly things. Don't be surprised if that is not the case right away. In fact, many feel the tug of worldly vices even greater after they accept Jesus Christ as their Lord and Savior. Connecting with a community of believers through a church can help direct your focus on Him. Like I said earlier, this is personal. You have to want this for your own life. Your pastor cannot do it for you. Your spouse cannot do it for you. In fact, your brother cannot do it for you. You have to make a choice and stick with it.

There is power in forgiveness. It frees the person offering the forgiveness. It can also make a way for healing to the person to whom the forgiveness is being offered. For most, forgiveness does not come easy. But it is essential.

I know what you're thinking. *But you don't know my story! You don't know what I have been through! There is no way I could ever forgive so-and-so for this! You don't know what you're talking about.* Maybe you're thinking, *Oh, I have moved in forgiveness; but, I will NEVER forget.*

I believe that for many of us, forgiveness can be a process. I also believe it is a behavior or a mindset that can be learned. Forgiveness is a choice. No matter how badly you have been victimized, mistreated, harmed, or hurt, you have the choice to move in forgiveness. I also want to remind you that there is power in forgiveness. Forgiveness first frees the person who was harmed – the victim. I have learned that forgiveness can also free the person to whom forgiveness is being given.

My act of forgiveness in the courtroom was more than just me releasing the hurt of the loss of Bobby and Pam. My act of forgiveness was a move that sought to remove any barrier to C.J. Martin being able to receive forgiveness. It burst open a door and probably made it just a little bit easier to accept the words that had been poured out over him from the very beginning of the accident.

I have talked with scores of people, and even wrote about one account in this book, about individual situations. I have heard how many have moved in forgiveness within their own heart, but never shared it with the other person. In many cases where we carry that burden, the other person may be living their life completely unaware that you are still carrying that. In some cases, simply telling the other person that you have forgiven them in a situation may result in that person being able to lay down a great weight.

But how can you forgive someone who isn't remorseful? That doesn't make any sense at all. If you believe in the Holy Bible, if you believe in Jesus Christ, here is a little reminder. He went to the cross for you (and me). *"But God commendeth his love toward us, in that, while we were yet sinners, Christ died for us." Romans 5:8 (KJV)* So, the Son of God, who became man, went to the cross to bear my sins, before I was even born, to make a way for me to get to heaven. It's personal! I have one more bombshell to drop on you. Think about this. God loves the person who you are harboring animosity towards every bit as much as He loves you. Try wrapping your mind around that. *"For God so loved the world..."* It doesn't say some of the world or, certain people in the world. He loves the whole world.

In the book of Matthew, Jesus Himself teaches us how to pray. He spells out a couple of verses that many of us learned as children. The Lord's Prayer is how Jesus teaches us how to pray. He talked to us about forgiveness in this prayer. In fact, in the first two verses after the prayer is addressed, Jesus speaks additionally about forgiveness.

"For if ye forgive men their trespasses, your heavenly Father will also forgive you; But if ye forgive not men their trespasses, neither will your Father forgive your trespasses." Matthew 6:14 – 15 (KJV)

In another scripture, the Apostle Peter asks Jesus how often we are to forgive. Look at what Jesus tell him, *"Then came Peter to Him (Jesus), and said, Lord, how oft shall my brother sin against me, and I forgive him? till seven times? Jesus saith unto him (Peter), I say not unto thee, Until seven times: but, Until seventy times seven." Matthew 18:21-22 (KJV)*

Forgiveness may not come easily. You may not even feel like forgiving. When we accept Jesus Christ as our Lord and Savior, ALL of our sin is forgotten. Satan will try to whisper about your past sins. The enemy will try to bring you down because of mistakes that you make. But, once you are forgiven by the Father, the sin is never remembered. You see, God doesn't say, "I'll forgive you. But, I will never forget." That is not how it works. It says in God's Word in *Micah 7:19 (KJV)*, *"He will turn again, he will have compassion upon us; he will subdue our iniquities; and thou wilt cast all their sins into the depths of the sea."* You see, God does not keep a record for those who have received the gift of salvation and are walking in accordance to His Will. We cannot harbor bad thoughts and ill-feelings toward someone we have forgiven.

Lastly, I want to talk about obedience. That word says so much about our faith, who we are as Christians, and what we believe. I used to say, "I just want to have a purpose. I want to know why I am here. What does God want me to do?" I would ask those questions, but I would never spend any time in His book to find the answers. Obedience requires humility. It is difficult, if not downright impossible, to be prideful and obedient. Obedience requires me to set my interests aside, to humble myself. I need to not be self-centered, but rather Christ-centered. I need to die to my self-interests more and more every day. I need less of me and more of Jesus in my life. I need to pick up my own cross, just as Jesus Christ had to do, and follow Him. Remember, what I am speaking about is a relationship. The relationship starts between you and Jesus and then grows from there.

Having a relationship with Jesus Christ is just the start. If we follow the teachings of Jesus Christ, then we are to love God the Father with everything that we are – all of our heart, soul, mind and strength. And we are to love our neighbor as ourselves. Well, that's simple enough, when I need to borrow some butter, my neighbor who lives in the house next door always gives me some. In this context, your neighbor includes many more than the people that live around you.

It is easy to love people who are like us. It is easy to love people who look like us; think like us; dress like us; vote like us; and love us back. It is much harder to love people who are different than us. When we walk in relationship with Jesus Christ, His love can be poured out through us. I know what I am talking about it. I am living it. Please know that I am not suggesting that I have perfected anything. I am just striving every day to walk in His righteousness.

The incredible thing is that people can see it in you. The scripture says that they will know you are disciples of Jesus by your love for one another. It seems to be a daily occurrence that someone will comment to me, "There's something different about you." I assure them that I wasn't always this way. I am being transformed as I am walking in love and moving toward obedience and forgiveness.

As you walk in love, you will find that you possess the other fruits of the Holy Spirit, too. In addition to love, these include joy, peace, longsuffering, gentleness, goodness, faith, meekness, and temperance. When you walk in faith and love and these other attributes begin to pour out, you will truly begin to understand the purpose you have here on earth. It essentially boils down to this:

Love God…Love People!

I wouldn't wish the things that have happened to me in my life on anyone else. But it would be absolutely wonderful if every person on the face of the earth could experience and receive the love of Jesus Christ into their life the way that I have.

As you reflect on what I have shared with you, especially in this chapter, I hope that your spirit has been stirred. If you read this book and you got to this point and the only thing you are thinking, is that this was an interesting story, then the entire point of the writing has been missed. It is my hope that you will be stirred to step into a relationship with Jesus Christ, or you will have a desire to move into a deeper relationship. I hope that you will be moved to action in the lives of the people who God brings across your path. I would hope that you would be willing to step out and step into the messes of other people's lives as God leads you. There are so many people who are hurting in this world. There is pure brokenness in our midst. And God is calling each of us to walk in obedience.

"Not any one of us can help everyone. But everyone can help someone. And that someone can be anyone."

Who will you help?

I am closing this chapter with this perspective. It came to me following a conversation that I had with C.J. in April 2018. He said something to me along the lines of, "You have told me, your brother's passing saved your life. Well, you showing up in the courtroom saved my life. I would like to think that I have been impacting your life ever since." After having a day or so to think on what he had said, I came to this realization:

"I have received far more from C.J. Martin than I have ever given to him."

Let that sink in for a moment.

"Judge not, and ye shall not be judged: condemn not, and ye shall not be condemned: forgive, and ye shall be forgiven: Give, and it shall be given unto you; good measure, pressed down, and shaken together, and running over, shall men give unto your bosom. For with the same measure that ye mete withal it shall be measured to you again."
Luke 6:37-38 (KJV)

Epilogue

What you have read in the preceding chapters is a testimony revealing how God can take our tragedies and turn them into triumphs. This was followed by a series of anecdotes and short stories that reveal the different ways that God moved through the lives of J.T. and Terri Lee Clark. And such stories are continuing to unfold. But this is only a part of the story.

As Terri Lee writes in one of the chapters, J.T. was not always this way. There was a very long period in their marriage when J.T. suffered greatly with depression and suicidal ideation. She endured a time where she did not know if he would arrive home at the end of the day. She raised their three children, not as a single mother, but burdened with the mental health issues of her husband.

As J.T. would suffer with and battle his depression, Terri Lee would serve as his personal prayer warrior. Even when he did not embrace this aspect of her life, she persisted nonetheless. There were times when he would push her away emotionally. He would say that she and the girls would be better off without him. In those times, she would hang on even tighter. She would remind him that when she took her marriage vows, she did so before her Lord and Savior. This was not something from which she could just walk away. She would later share that many would encourage her to leave J.T. She didn't deserve this, and she shouldn't have to put up with his condition. While she acknowledged the challenges of it. She knew she could not quit.

Terri Lee has a powerful and compelling story that she shares when she is invited to speak at churches, women's groups, and other venues. She talks about her faith and how she sustained it. She shares how God was able to work through her to help her husband. Her speaking engagements have encouraged hundreds of women who have heard her speak.

Terri Lee looks forward to sharing more of her story on this fascinating journey. As J.T. is often heard saying, the testimony you just read would not have happened without her testimony.

Appendix

CROSS & BRANCHES

In association with doves, the olive tree branch is a traditional symbol of peace and hope in many religions, descending from its role in Baptisms and the story of Noah and the Flood.

The branches form the shape of a cross, symbolizing christianity and the ministry. Furthermore, the leaves and lines of the cross are positioned to reflect the directional shape of the collision path that tragically took Bobby & Pam's life. The lines of the cross also never meet in the center, representing the fact that the vehicles never collided

DOVES

Doves are perhaps the most recognized symbol of hope and peace. They are also symbolic of messengers.

PAM

COLOR

The combination of Blue and Brown represent the earth and the sky, and the connection between heaven and us on Earth.

OUTER CIRCLE

The logo is circular in shape, symbolizing how everything in life comes full-circle. This signifies how everyone has come together, and in the case of this tragedy, it has ultimately concluded in love and forgiveness. The boldness and solidarity of the outer circle represents the overall restoration and healing of those involved.

The outer circle has uneven edges, not only giving the effect of paint on rough asphalt, but also providing an element of imperfection. No person or thing is absolutely perfect, and mistakes should be forgiven.

BOBBY

DASHED LINE

The dashed line in combination with the outer circle depicts the painted lines on a road, representing the setting where the tragedy occured. This line symbolizes the brokenness of the moment.

MY BROTHERS' CROSSING

"Brothers'" is written in the plural possessive form and is not actually intended to be a reference to Bobby Clark, the brother of JT Clark (Co-creator of My Brothers' Crossing). In fact, it is not even intended to apply only to men. This grammar is meant to apply to all of us that have been impacted or touched by the tragedy and God's movement through it all – Martin Family, Quesinberry Family, Clark Family, T.R.A.S.H. and H.O.P Ministries; the trooper; first responders; witnesses; and all who have heard the story and a message of love and hope, obedience and forgiveness.

About the Authors

J.T. and Terri Lee Clark live in Boones Mill, Virginia. They are parents to three daughters, Jordan, Caitlin, and Whitney. J.T. works full-time for a federally-funded healthcare coalition known as the Near Southwest Preparedness Alliance (NSPA). NSPA exists primarily to help regional healthcare interests prepare for, respond to, and recover from disasters. At the time of the accident, J.T. served as the executive director of the coalition. In May 2016, he stepped down from this role to a staff role to allow more time for ministry.

J.T.'s current career pursuits follow a long career in healthcare where he worked as a director of facilities management for three different hospitals. Prior to that he was a firefighter/EMT. He and his wife served as volunteers in the community where they lived when they met. In fact, that is how they met, through the volunteer fire/EMS.

Terri Lee, formerly a paramedic/firefighter, currently volunteers as an EMT with Red Valley Rescue Squad in Franklin County. She also serves as a volunteer with the Near Southwest Medical Reserve Corps.

Together, J.T. and Terri Lee operate a ministry known as My Brothers' Crossing. This ministry was borne of the tragedy that claimed the lives of J.T.'s brother, Bobby, and Bobby's wife, Pam. Through this ministry, J.T. and Terri Lee travel to venues to share a message of love, hope, forgiveness, unity, grace, mercy, and obedience. They are often heard saying, "We will go wherever He makes a way." To date, they have never asked to speak anywhere, but the invitations continue to come. Terri Lee speaks about her steadfastness through J.T.'s battles with depression and suicidal ideation. She talks about her decision to remain committed throughout a marriage that has lasted more than 30 years.

In addition to speaking, teaching, and preaching opportunities, they are both involved in prison ministry; visitation to the sick, injured, and infirmed at healthcare facilities and to those who are homebound; Terri Lee is a medical provider; involved in community outreach and evangelism; helping the homeless and the hungry; raising money to support emergency management scholarships;

amongst other initiatives. Additionally, they both serve as chaplains for Franklin County Public Safety. In this capacity, they respond to emergency calls upon dispatch to provide comfort and connect people with resources. This includes citizens, first responders, and other healthcare workers.

When they are not traveling as part of their ministry operations, they attend T.R.A.S.H. Ministry on Friday nights. They attend House of Purpose Ministries on Sundays. They also attend Bible study on Wednesday nights.

In addition to their three daughters, they are parents to a black lab, Maya. They also have three cats, Silver, Mocha, and Meeko.

Contact Information

My Brothers' Crossing, Inc.
P.O. Box 270
Boones Mill, VA 24065

Terri Lee Clark
Founder, Servant Leader
(540) 352-8815
terri.lee.clark@mybrotherscrossing.org

J.T. Clark
Founder, Servant Leader, Minister
(540) 986-6106
jt.clark@mybrotherscrossing.org

Facebook: @mybrotherscrossing
Instagram: my_brothers_crossing
Website: www.mybrotherscrossing.org

CPSIA information can be obtained
at www.ICGtesting.com
Printed in the USA
LVHW022002070619
620590LV00002B/4/P

9 781640 881457